HOW TO LIVE
KOREAN

HOW TO LIVE KOREAN

Soo Kim

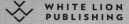

WHITE LION
PUBLISHING

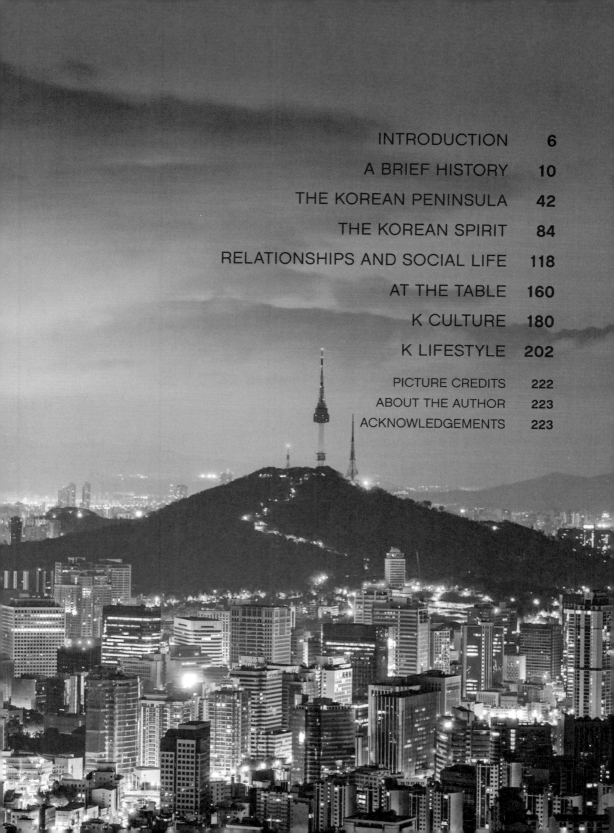

Introduction

All things Korean, from music and film to food, design and technology, have burst onto the world stage in recent years and South Korea is certainly having a moment. This ancient country has come into the 21st-century limelight with *hallyu* (Korean Wave), the rise of the popularity of South Korean culture, reaching a crescendo in the last decade.

But before I go on, you must be warned – this isn't just a run-of-the-mill cultural travel guide on where to go and what to see in South Korea. The Korean peninsula is much more complex than what these material barometers can measure and, as Aristotle said, the whole is greater than the sum of its parts.

From kimchee to K-pop and everything in between, this book will unpack what it means to be Korean in all its forms, through the unfiltered eyes of a Korean native who has been immersed in a Korean upbringing and cultural setting for nearly 40 years.

The only way to truly know a person is to walk a mile in their shoes. So, here I will take you on a journey through the heart and soul of South Korea, with a few stops along the way, uncovering the way Koreans think, feel, act and ultimately live their lives.

To truly understand how and why people think, act and feel the way they do, it's important to trace their origins and follow their story from the past to the present. Here, I will walk you through the rich and diverse history of the Korean peninsula which has created the modern shape of the region today.

RIGHT: Illuminated buildings at nighttime in Seoul.

I will also explain the character and essence of Koreans – how they behave, relate to and interact with one another and others – and dissect the day-to-day life of Koreans, from family customs, traditions and cultural norms to what family, friendships, dating and marriage mean and entail in Korean society.

Food is at the heart of Korean communities and there's been an explosion of Korean cuisine on the global food scene. The South Korean capital Seoul gained a Michelin Guide in 2016 and now boasts a growing list of Michelin-starred restaurants. This book will trace the evolution of Korean dining customs and eating and drinking culture in Korea, as well as explore the country's most quintessential dishes.

Whether it be fashion, beauty, celebrities or social media, there is no doubt that Koreans are passionate people with many interests. They take pride in their history and how far they've come but they're always looking for the next best thing. It's this spirit of both perseverance and innovation that have been the key ingredients of South Korea's success and continued rise on an economic, cultural and societal level.

With that in mind, I hope this journey through one of Asia's most fascinating and sophisticated countries inspires you, at the very least, to do and be passionate just the same, while hopefully showing you a thing or two about how to live Korean.

RIGHT: A table filled with a variety of Korean food.

A Brief History

The early dynasty eras

What's in a name? An incredible ancient history in the case of Korea, whose past is permanently etched into its name. The term Korea stems from the name Koguryŏ (also spelled Goguryeo), one of the earliest kingdoms of Korea, which later evolved to become Koryŏ (or Goryeo).

Life on the Korean peninsula can be traced as far back as the Paleolithic and Neolithic Ages. Several excavated sites across the peninsula today indicate that the earliest inhabitants used tools made from animal horns to hunt during the Paleolithic period, while from around 8,000 BC, the use of more polished stone tools and farming began. These were the most primitive beginnings of a region that would later be ruled by kingdoms.

While these early clans formed the peninsula's first settlements, its distinctly Korean cultural roots were planted in the first century with the founding of the Three Kingdoms – the Koguryŏ kingdom in the north around 37 BC and two other kingdoms in the south (Baekjae in the southwest and Silla in the southeast, which formed around 18 BC and 57 BC respectively).

After Baekjae and Koguryŏ were conquered by Silla, the peninsula was ruled under a Unified Silla kingdom from 668 AD. It was the first kingdom that brought the peninsula under a unified rule, until around 698 AD when the Balhae kingdom was founded and began ruling the north of the peninsula and parts of Manchuria.

Buddhist and Confucian influences

The Unified Silla period was an extensive period of growth for the arts in the peninsula. Having maintained close ties with the Tang Dynasty of China (618–907 AD), the country drew much from Chinese culture, including Chinese Buddhism which had a significant influence on Korean culture, especially in architecture, during the Silla period.

The oldest Buddhist stones, carvings, temples and tombs in South Korea, including the Bulguksa Temple (a UNESCO World Heritage Site) as well as the Hwangnyongsa Temple and the Bunhwangsa Temple in the city of Gyeongju, are from the Silla period and showcase the architecture of the era.

RIGHT: Statue of King Seongjong, the sixth ruler of the Koryŏ kingdom, in Seoul.

Confucianism

This ancient school of thought is associated with the teachings of Chinese philosopher Confucius (the Latin form of the Mandarin Chinese name Kǒng Fūzǐ), who lived from 551 to 479 BC. It was established as China's official state ideology during the Han Dynasty (206 BC to 220 AD).

Humanism, the development of the self, both individually and collectively in society, forms the heart of Confucianism. Confucius was a strong believer in what's known as the Golden Rule, which states: 'Do not do unto others what you do not want done to yourself.' This concept of reciprocity and moral obligation is fundamental to Confucian beliefs.

Confucianism focuses on practicality rather than spirituality, and self-actualisation through rituals and relationships in everyday life rather than questions of existentialism, gods and the afterlife. It teaches that harmony and social order are maintained when people fulfill defined social and ethical roles, be it through devotion to their parents or loyalty to the government and other acts.

Confucius's teachings were outlined in a collection of scriptures known as the Chinese classics, which include the Five Classics and Four Books. These scriptures contained the roots of some of the enduring principles of Korean culture, including filial piety (a virtue of utmost respect for your parents, elders as well as rulers), which formed the core of Confucian beliefs.

Neo-Confucianism was an updated later version of the Confucian teachings which took prominence in Korea during the Koryŏ and Joseon dynasties.

Along with Buddhism, Confucianism was another Chinese import that began to take shape on the peninsula in this era. It was considered to be the main philosophy followed by members of the aristocracy. By around 682 AD, a Confucian school was formed and its entry was restricted to society's elite aristocrats.

Expansion of culture and the arts

The Koryŏ Dynasty was first formed around 918 AD when the country was in a period of national unrest and division from around 892 to 935 AD, with three states collectively known as the Later Three Kingdoms (consisting of the Silla, Hubaekjae and Hugoguryeo kingdoms) each pushing against a weakening Unified Silla rule, which was sparked by the excessive taxation of the people.

The Koryŏ Dynasty fully established its control and unified the peninsula again around 935 AD, leading to the demise of the Unified Silla kingdom following nearly a 1,000 year rule.

The Koryŏ Dynasty was marked by an extensive flourishment of the arts. Some of the country's most intricate works in lacquerware and stoneware, stylised with designs unique to Korea, originated from this period.

The kingdom also experienced economic growth during this ancient era, trading with both China and Japan and exporting gold, silver, ginseng, cotton, as well as *hanji* paper (a type of handmade paper made from mulberry trees produced in Korea). It was known for its white colour, strength and texture.

The influence of Buddhism remained, with several kings, other members of royalty and the nobility being Buddhists and entering monkhood. While Buddhism was still the state religion, the principles of Confucianism began to shape government structure. In the latter half of the Koryŏ Dynasty, Buddhism's influence declined, with the introduction of Neo-Confucianism – a school of thought rejecting the mystical elements of Buddhism and favouring a more rational ethical philosophy.

By around 958 AD, King Gwangjo, the fourth king of the Koryŏ kingdom, established *gwageo* – a national civil service examination which was based on China's civil service examinations administered under the Tang Dynasty.

ABOVE: A colourful painting in the Pohyon-sa Korean Buddhist temple, Mount Myohyang, North Korea.

The exam tested one's writing skills and knowledge of the Chinese classics (which were of the Neo-Confucian tradition).

King Seongjong, the sixth ruler of the Koryŏ kingdom, also supported Confucianism and promoted the separation of religion and government. He later established the *gukjagam* in 992 AD, the highest institution of education in the country of the period – a school for scholars, which provided training in the Chinese classics.

The beginnings of a Korean identity

After nearly 1,000 years, the Koryŏ kingdom ended and the Joseon Dynasty began in 1392. After around five centuries, it became Korea's last kingdom and the longest ruling Confucian dynasty. During this period, Confucianism was fully established as the state ideology.

Following invasions from Japan and Manchuria in the late 16th and early 17th centuries, the country maintained an isolationist foreign policy, refusing any trade with the West and trading at very limited capacity with China and Japan, and was known as the 'Hermit Kingdom.'

This period of isolation also saw immense cultural growth in the country. It was a golden age for Korean painting (establishing a distinctive Korean style of painting, moving towards realism and away from the idealisation of landscapes that was prominent among Chinese artists). It was also the peninsula's greatest period of scientific advancement, with the invention of an automated water clock and celestial globes that indicated the positions of the sun, moon and stars and seasonal variations.

The legacy of the Joseon Dynasty can be seen in modern-day Korea, from traditional Korean tea ceremonies to structures of architectural interest including fortresses and palaces that were introduced in the Joseon era. The kingdom planted the beginnings of what would form the foundation of Korean society for centuries to come, from local provincial governments and social classes (such as *yangban*, a group given nobility status by passing the *gwageo* and who later became government officials) to the creation of the Korean language and the establishment of Hanyang (which is modern-day Seoul) as the country's capital.

ABOVE: Deoksugung Palace, the royal palace of the Joseon Dynasty, in Seoul.

Japanese occupation

Following a series of wars that saw Japan, China and Russia battle it out for control over Korea, the struggle was finally won by Japan. A treaty outlining permanent trade agreements and diplomatic relations between Korea and Japan was established in 1876, without restrictions from either country. The treaty included a clause that granted Japan extraterritoriality in Korea, which effectively gave the Japanese free reign in Korea, so any crimes they committed would essentially have no consequences. Korea was forced to agree to these unfair terms following the demonstration of Japan's military power in a series of Japanese gunboat attacks on the Korean islands of Ganghwa and Yeongjong in 1875.

From 1897, just after the end of the Joseon Dynasty, the peninsula was briefly unified as the Korean Empire before Japan fully colonised the country from 1910 to 1945.

Korea, historically an agricultural economy, underwent an industrial revolution under the Japanese regime. The country saw rapid urban growth following the arrival of the steel, chemical and hydroelectric power industries under Japanese rule. Japan built infrastructure throughout the country in the form of roads, railroads and ports, in addition to electrical power and government buildings, all of which helped to modernise Korea.

The country was the second-most industrialised nation in Asia, after Japan, by the end of the Japanese occupation period in 1945. Many of the methods of economic development implemented by Japan during this time were adopted by South Korea in the 1960s.

ABOVE: The Japanese army in Seoul, November 1894, after the victory at Asan, during the Sino-Japanese War.

The suppression of Korean culture

While the Japanese colonial era sparked industrial development in the country, it was also a period of extreme dominance. From the removal of Korean language and history from school curriculums to pressuring Koreans to change their names to Japanese ones, the Japanese authorities clamped down on Korean identity and culture. At one point it was even illegal to speak Korean, while more than nearly 75,000 artefacts were estimated to have been taken from Korea by Japan.

Koreans were made to worship Japanese Shinto shrines, abandoning the country's religious beliefs, which had included Christianity introduced by Western missionaries. Several Christians were persecuted during this period and churches were burned by Japanese soldiers.

These years of oppression led to the rise of anti-Japan rallies such as the March 1st Movement in 1919, the most public and large-scale series of protests against foreign domination in Korean history, and which served as the catalyst for the Korean Independence Movement.

March 1st saw nearly 2 million people participate in more than 1,500 protests across the country, with leaders in different areas reading aloud a declaration of Korean independence in public, proclaiming Koreans would no longer tolerate Japanese oppression. The protests entailed peaceful processions, but were met by violent suppression from Japanese authorities who deployed military forces to push back against the crowds, resulting in the death of nearly 8,000 Koreans, around 16,000 wounded and nearly 47,000 arrested by Japanese officials.

The March 1st protests were followed by a very slight easing of strict Japanese pressures in the form of civilian forces replacing military police and the permission of freedom of the press on a restricted level. Two of the country's biggest newspapers in history, the *Dong-a-Ilbo* and the *Chosun Ilbo*, were launched around this period.

However, anti-Japanese sentiment and the desire for Korean independence remained strong. On 1 April 1919 the Korean Provisional Government, a government-in-exile based in Shanghai, was set up by Ahn Chang Ho and Syngman Rhee, the leaders of the Korean National Association, a political group launched in 1909 by Korean natives based abroad determined to fight Japanese oppression and colonisation of the Korean peninsula.

Ahn later founded the New Korea Society (Shinminhoe), one of the most significant clandestine groups to fight Japanese occupation, while Rhee later became the first president of South Korea in 1948.

The suffering and deaths of many Koreans during this period of brutal suppression left a legacy of animosity and deep-rooted sense of injustice among Koreans when it comes to their feelings towards the Japanese, some of which has carried over into modern times across generations.

PREVIOUS PAGE: People take part in a ceremony marking the 100th anniversary of the March 1st Movement against Japanese colonial occupation in Seoul, in 2019.

Kim Jung Yong

From clandestine grassroots movements within the peninsula to immigrants abroad, thousands of Korean activists have helped shape the modern age of South Korea today. Among these revolutionaries was a man of humble beginnings with big dreams from the south of the country called Kim Jung Yong – or better known to me as my late grandfather.

Born in 1906 in the southern province of Gyeungsangbukdo, my grandfather grew up in the Japanese colonial era and witnessed the height of the oppression. He joined the independence efforts during his studies abroad: one of the few who had managed to receive university education outside of Korea, he studied first in Japan and then at Maryville College in Tennessee, US.

While in the US, he was mentored by Ahn Chang Ho and worked closely with Syngman Rhee for the cause of Korean independence. During one of his covert missions, my grandfather's cover was blown on a journey by sea to Korea when a Korean national flag was discovered in his briefcase. He was arrested in Shanghai and imprisoned in Japan where he was tortured and remained until the end of Japanese occupation in 1945 when he was released back to Korea.

Upon his return, being one of the few English-speaking Koreans in the country, he worked as an interpreter for the government during the brief period of US military occupation that followed Japan's colonial rule. He spent his later years as an influential public official and as an English professor at different schools in Daegu before he passed away in 1965.

My grandfather was given two national honours by two past presidents of South Korea for his services. He is buried in Daejeon National Cemetery, which honours Korean veterans and revolutionaries. There on grave No 52, written in stone is my grandfather's name, along with mine, that of my grandmother, his sons, their wives and children and a summary of his work in the independence movement. My grandmother, too, was laid to rest here next to my grandfather with military honours.

The north–south split

Following Japan's surrender to the Allied Forces in 1945 at the end of the Second World War, the country struggled to form a unified government given the diverging ideologies between the North and South. By 1948, the peninsula was divided at the 38th parallel, between the Soviet-occupied North and US-occupied South and tension increased across the peninsula, as both sides claimed to represent the interests and ideology of the entire country.

On 25 June 1950, the Northern forces, backed by Soviet weapons and a Chinese army, invaded the South which sparked the Korean War. The war ended with a ceasefire that established the Demilitarized Zone (DMZ) which has been in place since July 1953. Running along the 38th parallel (latitude 38°N), this marks the official demarcation line between North and South Korea, with military forces pulled back for around 1.2 miles (2km) from the line on both sides. The area spans 150 miles (240km) across the peninsula, from the mouth of the Han River in the west to just south of the North Korean town of Kosŏng in the east.

However, this armistice agreement was never actually signed by South Korea, due to Rhee's strong opposition towards the negotiations, which were initiated by the US, and his subsequent refusal to sign the agreement. The armistice was signed only by Chinese military officials, the North and the United Nations Command military force 'on behalf of the international community'. There was no peace treaty signed, so technically the North and South are still at war as of today.

Diverging ideologies

While the North and South share a common historical and cultural background, the government and economic system of both halves grew dramatically different. The North was heavily influenced by that of the Soviet Union and China, with a centralised political system led by the late Kim Il Sung, the grandfather of North Korea's current leader Kim Jong Un, who is known as 'The Great Leader' among North Koreans. The North developed its own politics based on *juche*, which translates to 'self-reliance', an ideology around economic and political independence. It went on to become one of the most

ABOVE LEFT: At the third tunnel from North Korea into South Korea in the demilitarized zone (DMZ).
BELOW LEFT: South Korean soldiers stand guard in the DMZ, facing North Korea.

closed communist states in the world, maintaining resistance to any reform despite the country's stark economic decline, even more than ten years after witnessing the collapse of the Soviet Union.

South Korea was much more influenced by the US – naturally, given America's historical involvement and intervention prior to the split – and operated by democratic values, at least in theory in some aspects.

South Korea's first president

Syngman Rhee was elected as South Korea's first president in 1948 and remained in office for three consecutive terms. Having had a broad university education at leading US universities, which included a Bachelor's degree at George Washington University, a Master's degree at Harvard University and a PhD at Princeton University, Rhee spoke fluent English and was a champion of American values including a strong anti-communist stance.

For these reasons, he was the favoured pick by the US military government for the transfer of power after the North–South split. Rhee was even featured on the cover of the global *Time* magazine in 1953, the year of the ceasefire between the North and South, with a subtitle that read: 'Korea's Syngman Rhee: Deep are the roots of freedom'.

But Rhee's presidency saw him assume dictatorial powers, shutting down any opposing parties and controlling the appointment of government officials including local officials such as mayors and chiefs of police. In 1960, after three consecutive re-elections, student demonstrations raged against Rhee's continued authoritarian rule and alleged rigged elections that year (which claimed Rhee had won the election by a 90 percent majority vote). The uprising eventually saw Rhee resign from office in 1960.

The birth of chaebols

Following Rhee's resignation, a coup in 1961 put Park Chung Hee in power, who ruled the country briefly under a military dictatorship before becoming the president in 1963.

Park's authoritarian presidency saw a radical shift in the country's outlook, establishing a protectionist policy, keeping foreign products from entering the country and facilitating an internally galvanised economy controlled by the state.

ABOVE: Portrait of Syngman Rhee, the first president of South Korea.

The era saw the rise of family-owned conglomerates known as *chaebols*, such as Hyundai, Samsung and LG, which today are among the leaders of Korea's export industry. These *chaebols* were fed by state incentives such as tax cuts, legality for their exploitative operations and other financial breaks.

This rapid export-driven economic growth and industrialisation led to the development of the Seoul subway system, a network of nationwide highways and other infrastructure within South Korea.

President Park remained in power until 1979 when he was assassinated and Chun Doo Hwan, became the next elected president. But the months leading to Chun's official appointment was another period of political turmoil that saw another round of protests.

National uprisings

Given his military background, before he was elected president, Chun held several commander positions within the armed forces, with the latest being director of the Korean Central Intelligence Agency. In 1980, before his election to the presidential office, by way of martial law, Chun placed restrictions on the press, banned political activities and closed universities across the country following rumours of North Koreans who had infiltrated the nation.

The move sparked swathes of public demonstrations, which were suppressed by the military using full force under Chun's orders. One such clash in the city of Gwangju led to a bloody massacre of hundreds of activists by military officials.

During his presidency, Chun attempted to operate a government that was different from Park's previous rule and hoped to eradicate the corrupt reputation that the government had developed under his predecessor. He made efforts to appeal to the public, in the form of introducing the broadcast of colour television across the nation, creating national baseball and football teams and reducing censorship on sexually suggestive films or television dramas.

It wasn't until the late 1980s, when the country began to see a market-oriented democracy that eventually transformed South Korea into a developed nation and in 1988, it hosted the Summer Olympics. In 1991, South Korea was formally invited to become a member of the United Nations and by 1997, the country began to transition from an autocracy into a modern democracy following the election of president Kim Dae Jung.

The modern age of South Korea

Walking past the pulsating neon-bright city lights of Myeongdong and Apgujeongdong, two of Seoul's busiest consumer areas, surrounded by towering skyscrapers at every corner of the capital, it's hard to believe that South Korea was a developing country only a few generations ago. The country has come a long way since its poverty-stricken days, especially after the Korean War and early 1960s, when it was deemed one of the world's poorest nations. Today, South Korea is the world's fourth largest urban economy and the twelfth biggest overall economy in the world, with a Gross Domestic Product (GDP) of around $1.62 trillion reported in 2018. Its rapid growth over a relatively short period of time has been referred to as the 'Miracle on the Han' – Han being the river that bisects the capital.

The keys to its growth has been its ongoing culture of innovation and a continued investment in research and development, which has been necessary to compete with the low labour costs of China and the well-established high-tech companies of Japan that have allowed production to thrive in those two rivalling neighbours.

While the South Korea of the 20th and 21st centuries has had its own milestones (in 2012, South Korea elected its first female president, Park Geun Hye, the daughter of former president Park) and more political strife (in 2016, Park was impeached following her link to corruption in government), which was preceded by another economic hurdle during the Asian financial crisis of the late 1990s, the country's modernisation soared into the 2000s.

A long way from its colonial era, South Korea has been a member of the Organisation for Economic Co-operation and Development (OECD) since 1996 and from November 2019, the country became a member of the OECD Development Committee, nearly half a century since it emerged from being one of the world's poorest countries. The country is also a member of other international financial bodies including the G20 and the Paris Club, a testament to South Korea's economic trajectory.

Today, with an ageing rural population and a farm labour shortage following urbanisation, less than a quarter of the country is farmed. The focus of the economy and its resources was shifted away from agriculture and directed to high-tech industries including automobiles, electronics and information technology. The *chaebol* conglomerates that were born in the mid-20th century thrive today as the country's leading companies, especially Hyundai and Samsung, which have both become global brands.

Booming automobile industry

South Korea's car industry has been growing exponentially since it first started manufacturing cars in around 1958, using US military jeep-type car parts to assemble its earliest models before its design and production techniques were further developed and refined.

Today, the country stands as the world's fifth largest producer of passenger cars, as home to some of the world's top-selling cars including Hyundai, Kia and Renault. South Korea is also leading the industry by way of green innovation in the car industry. Back in 2013, Hyundai unveiled the world's first commercially mass-produced hydrogen fuel-cell electric vehicle (FCEV) – the Hyundai Tucson FCEV. The government hopes to produce 6.3 million FCEVs and 1,200 refuelling stations in South Korea by 2040, in a bid to reduce carbon emissions. By 2018, around 32,000 FCEVs were supplied in South Korea.

In other automobile innovations, SoCar (South Korea's leading car-sharing company, which allows users to book cars by the hour or day at designated zones) is collaborating with a string of leading tech companies including Tesla, SK Telecom and Naver to merge self-driving and car-sharing technologies and create a new type of vehicle exchange system. SoCar has been a success in South Korea, with nearly 6.4 million using the car-sharing app and the company is now offering more than 10,000 cars for hire.

LEFT: Shoppers and nightlife among the streets of Myeongdong, Seoul, South Korea.
NEXT PAGE: Hyundai Motor Co. vehicles bound for export await shipment at a port near the company's Ulsan plant.

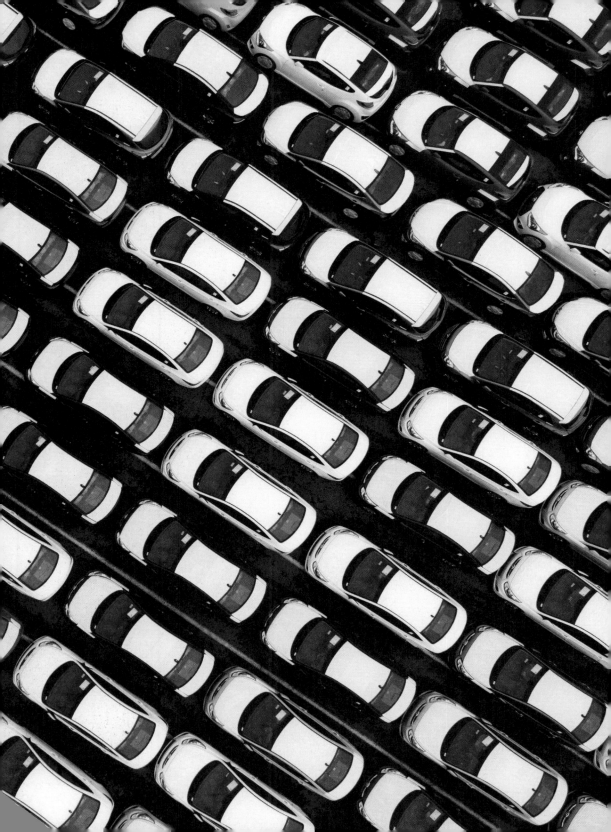

State-of-the-art technology

One of South Korea's most impressive technological advances has been in the electronics industry, especially within mobile phones and telecommunications. Its success begs the chicken or the egg question of whether the country's fast-moving mobile industry has created digital phone addiction among teenagers and others or vice versa. But there's no question about South Korea's advancement of the technology industry. Locals half-jokingly say that people in South Korea change phones as frequently as they would socks, because new models with advanced features are introduced so quickly.

The country's leading electronics company is by far Samsung, which is the world's second largest technology company, just after Apple, and the world's largest manufacturer of mobile phones, smartphones and televisions. Samsung was originally founded as a grocery trading company but entered the electronics business in the 1960s during the Park presidency, when the government backed these family-run conglomerates. It has since been South Korea's largest *chaebol* company and today is among the top ten global brands in the world, having maintained its top-ranking position in the global television market for ten consecutive years in 2015. Some of Samsung's biggest innovations in recent years include the world's first 3D LED screen for a movie theatre, the world's first smartphone with a curved edge screen and the world's first curved as well as bendable televisions.

In April 2019, South Korea became the first to offer country-wide 5G service for mobile phone networks, allowing users to connect 20 times faster than on a 4G network. With the launch of nationwide 5G, came the launch of Samsung's Galaxy S10 phone, which became the first 5G phone in South Korea.

RIGHT: **People wear virtual reality devices for an audio-visual experience at KT Corp's 5G Bus in Seoul, January 2019.**

10 things you never knew about South Korea

1. It has more than 3,000 islands

There are around 3,300 islands to be explored in South Korea, including Bijindo, off the coast of the port city of Tongyeong in the southern province of Gyeongsangnamdo. Visitors can view the sunrise and sunset from the same spot on a beach that connects two islands. The country's longest beach coast, stretching for 8 miles (12km), can be found on Imjado in the Jeollanamdo province in the south.

2. It has the fastest internet on the planet

Tech junkies in South Korea can get their internet fix faster than anywhere else in the world. In November 2019, the country recorded the world's fastest mobile internet connection speed, according to the latest Speedtest Global Index, nearly four times quicker than the average speed in other countries. South Korea's fixed broadband internet connection speed was reported to be more than twice as fast as the global average, while in 2017 the country had the world's fastest internet speed for the 12th consecutive quarter in the annual international State of the Internet report from the US-based content platform Akamai. But its need for digital speed doesn't stop there. The South Korean government also revealed its plan to offer 10Gb (gigabit) internet, which is ten times faster than Gigabit internet, the fastest internet service currently available. The country hopes to offer 10Gb to 50 percent of the global population by around 2022.

RIGHT: Looking out to Seongsan Ilchulbong, Jeju Island.

3. ... and created the world's first social media network

Before there was Facebook, Instagram or Twitter, there was Cyworld, which was launched in South Korea in 1999 and redeveloped in 2001. Roughly similar to MySpace, which launched a few years later, Cyworld was the earliest form of a mass social networking service (SNS) that allowed users to have avatars and virtual rooms, which they could decorate to their taste using virtual furniture and other elements to represent their profile. Its initial version was much more basic and simply provided a list of members and their contact details to allow users to connect offline. The network's name refers to cyber but also references the Korean word 사이 (pronounced 'sye'), which means relationship, underscoring its basic premise to foster relationships within a local community.

4. ... and the first internet café

As early as 1988, two Koreans opened a very basic cybercafé of sorts with two 16-bit computers connected to the internet via a telephone line, just opposite Hongik University in Seoul. Later, in 1994, the modern-day internet café, known as a 'PC bang' in Korean (*bang* being the Korean word for 'room'), was born. These PC bangs played a crucial role in the launch of gaming culture and the computer-based online game market, which took off in the late 1990s.

5. It's the breakdancing capital of the world

While many may be familiar with K-pop, not many have heard of South Korea's other popping passion. The lock-and-pop street dance hailing from the US hip-hop music scene took South Korea by storm after it was introduced to the country via the American Forces Network, the broadcast channel serving the US military with American programmes. From the 1990s, the music-crazed youth of South Korea latched onto breakdancing, which was a regular feature on the network. Around a decade later, South Korea joined the ranks of the Battle of the Year international breakdancing competition and Korean breakdancers have been awarded nearly 20 titles since, including seven first place wins between 2002 and 2018. In addition, Korean b-boy and b-girl crews bagged several second- and third-place titles and best show awards over the 30-year span of the annual dance championship.

ABOVE: Breakdancer Jong Ho 'Leon' Kim of Korea performs as other B-Boys watch on.

6. Koreans are related to Russians

The genetic makeup of Koreans has been linked to people from Siberia's Lake Baikal region, as well as parts of Central Asia, indigenous Southeast Asia, Mongolia and the coastal areas around the Yellow Sea. In 2017, genetic studies of bones in the Far East of Russia found that modern-day Koreans are related to people who have lived in Russia's Primorsky Krai region for around 8,000 years.

7. … and are pioneers of the printing process

Movable metal type printing was first used in Korea in the early 13th century during the Koryŏ dynasty. The first book made using a metal movable type printing process – *Jikji* (a book of Buddhism teachings) – was produced in 1377, nearly a century before the process was introduced in Europe by Johannes Gutenberg around 1439, where it was further developed and ignited the mass printing industry.

8. It produced the world's first newspaper

The oldest newspaper in the world was reportedly printed in South Korea, according to a Buddhist monk from the Yonghwa Temple in the Gyeongsangbukdo province who claims to have five issues of the *Jobo*, a Korean daily newspaper, dating back to November 1577. The existence of the *Jobo* was first documented in 1508 in the UNESCO-listed historical script known as Silok (The Annals of the Joseon Dynasty), which covers the longest period of a single dynasty. The paper, which reported on the ruling king at the time and other palace news including the appointment of officials, was said to have been short-lived after King Seonjo cut its publication, angered that matters of the royal court were being publicised outside the palace.

9. … and was the earliest cultivator of rice

The oldest-ever grain of rice, which is now consumed by more than half of the world's population, was found to be in the South Korean province of Chungcheongbukdo, according to research by archaeologists in Korea. Back in 2003, burnt rice grains dating back 15,000 years were discovered in the village of Sorori by scientists, the earliest sign of rice cultivation.

10. There's a train connecting North and South Korea

The Dorasan Station, which sits about 35 miles (56km) from Seoul and 128 miles (205km) from the North Korean capital Pyongyang, was built in 2002 during the presidency of Kim Dae Jung, which saw some improvement in relations between the North and South. It once saw freight trains travel daily between the Kaesong Industrial Complex in the North to Dorasan Station. But following renewed tension between the two countries, it was effectively shut down in 2008 and remains a disused railway station serving as a tourist attraction. The station can be reached from Seoul on the Gyeongui Line and is the last stop of the railway line.

ABOVE: Akyang rice paddy field, Hadong, Gyeongsangnamdo.

The Korean
Peninsula

Jeollanamdo

Jeju

Provinces

South Korea is divided into nine main provinces, which include Chungcheongbukdo, Chungcheongnamdo, Gangwondo, Gyeonggido, Gyeongsangbukdo, Gyeongsangnamdo, Jeollabukdo, Jeollanamdo and the Jeju Special Self-Governing Province.

Within these provinces, there are eight administrative divisions designated as 'Special Cities' which are at the same level as provinces. These cities include Seoul, Busan, Incheon, Daegu, Daejeon, Gwangju, Sejong and Ulsan.

South Korea covers about 45 percent of the peninsula, while North Korea occupies the remainder. There are also five northern provinces governed by South Korea that are located entirely in North Korea. The five northern provinces are Hwanghaedo, Pyeongannamdo, Pyeonganbukdo, Hamkyeongnamdo and Hamkyeongbukdo.

The borders of these provinces in the north were established during the Japanese occupation period in 1945 and remain from that era. They are governed by South Korea's Committee for the Five Northern Korean Provinces, which is part of South Korea's Ministry of Interior and Safety. The committee provides administrative support to the five northern provinces, which are home to around 8.5 million people.

These five northern provinces are not part of North Korea's official nine provinces, which include Chagang, North Hamgyong, South Hamgyong, North Hwanghae, South Hwanghae, Kangwon, North Pyongan, South Pyongan and Ryanggang.

RIGHT: **Seoraksan National Park in Gangwondo province.**

Seoul

The country's capital Seoul is categorised as a provincial level 'Special City', known as the Seoul Capital Area. But geographically, Seoul sits at the heart of the Gyeonggido province. The Seoul Capital Area also consists of the city of Incheon and the Gyeonggido province.

The bustling South Korean capital has a dizzying array of culture on offer with a fascinating slice of Korean life to be explored at every corner. Its busy streets form a transfixing technicolour display of neon-lit shops beckoning you to a cornucopia of pleasure grounds from *norehbangs* (karaoke bars), *PC bangs* (internet/gaming cafes) and *jjimjilbangs* (Korean bathhouses or spas) to *pojangmachas* (street-food tents and stalls) and every type of chicken and *galbi* (Korean beef ribs) restaurant you could wish for, permeated by an equally colourful clan of creatives, fashionistas and hipster-types.

Always switched-on in one way or another, the city's finger-on-the-pulse feel is evident among everyone and everywhere, including underground where I have seen even ageing grandmothers, holding giant baskets of vegetables looking like they've literally just come from harvesting in the fields, glued to a smartphone on the metro (which, of course, is Wi-Fi connected).

But the true beauty of the capital is in its juxtaposition of the old and new, as home to both the most futuristic buildings in the world as well as historic treasures including temples, shrines and palaces. Walking and breathing these grounds of living history offers a true step back in time right in the heart of the city, not just in presence but also in ritual: at Gyeongbokgung Palace, visitors can witness a daily re-enactment of the changing of the guards from the Joseon Dynasty, featuring a ceremonial procession at its main gate (the Gwanghamun) led by guards dressed in full traditional guard attire of the Joseon era.

Enclosed by four mountains and bisected by the meandering Han River, Seoul forms the urban centre of the country, with nearly 10 million people crossing each other's paths. In order to help relieve congestion in Seoul, the 'Special Autonomous City' of Sejong was founded in 2007 to serve as a new national 'mini-capital'. Several government ministries have been relocated to this area. Sejong is among the least populous regions of the country but the government aims to bring the population up to around 500,000 by 2030.

ABOVE LEFT: Gyeongbokgung Palace in Seoul. ABOVE RIGHT: Illuminated street signs in the city. BELOW: A busy crosswalk in Seoul.

Seoul neighbourhoods

Gangnam

Sitting just below the Han River, Gangnam literally means 'south of the river' in Korean. The area, and the country as a whole, was put back on the world map following the success of the song 'Gangnam Style' by the South Korean rapper/singer Psy, who is from the Gangnam District, born to a wealthy family.

The district was once the least developed part of the capital, but over the last 30–40 years it has seen immense development, making it the richest part of the country. The luxury district offers the most expensive real estate in South Korea, dotted with the homes of many celebrities and other public figures, from K-pop artists and movie stars to politicians. Most of South Korea's biggest entertainment agencies, including JYP Entertainment, FNC and Polaris, are headquartered here, as are the biggest tech companies and international businesses such as Google, IBM and Toyota.

The phrase 'Gangnam style', as noted in the song by Psy, refers to the wealth and trendy lifestyle associated with residents of this upper class area.

ABOVE: **Designer storefronts in the modern business and shopping district of Gangnam.**

The population of this small district makes up only around one percent of the country's total population of around 51.5 million.

Gangnam's most popular neighbourhoods include Cheongdamdong, Apgujeongdong and Sinsadong, all dripping with extravagance and housing the most upmarket fashion boutiques, hotels, bars, restaurants and nightclubs in the city.

Apgujeongdong's Rodeo Street is known as the 'Beverly Hills of Korea', comparing it with the Los Angeles neighbourhood for its collection of brand-name shops and beauty salons frequented by a star-studded celebrity crowd. Garosugil in Sinsadong is a tree-lined street featuring several designer stores, boutiques and cafes where celebrities are often spotted, while Cheongdamdong offers more of the same, as home to several international luxury brands including Prada, Louis Vuitton, Burberry and Cartier, among others.

But beyond the money and fame, Gangnam has become one of the country's main business hubs. Recently, it began to host some major world events such as the G20 Summit and Nuclear Security Summit in 2010 and 2012.

ABOVE: The Galleria Department Store, Seoul's most popular luxury-brand fashion mall, in Gangnam.

Hongdae

This trendy area of Seoul is named after Hongik University (*Hongik daehak* in Korean, where the shortened term Hongdae comes from), a prestigious art college in the Mapogu district. Mapogu is home to several universities, including Ewha Women's University – another elite school, as well as government buildings.

Crawling with students and a sprinkling of curious tourists, the area has a buzzy vibe throughout the day and night, drawing a cool, young crowd around its quirky cafes, hole-in-the-wall bars, bakeries and bustling restaurants.

Its hipster roots come from its days as a haven for musicians and other artist-types in the 1990s, who flocked there for the cheap rent at the time. Today, the area is also home to several wealthy public figures such as the chairman of Samsung.

Hongdae forms the home of the underground Korean indie music scene and its legacy remains with several annual music festivals hosted in the neighbourhood. Its streets are teeming with music from buskers and venues including the Hongdae Playground, an outdoor live music, flea market and exhibition space near the entrance of the university, showcasing indie music acts and works from local artists.

Hongdae is also known for its clubbing scene; on Live Club Day, which is held on the last Friday of every month, you gain access to various nightclubs with one wristband.

For a break from the busy streets of Hongdae, head to nearby Yeonnamdong, an up-and-coming trendy hotspot among students and artists. Often referred to as 'the quieter Hongdae', its alleyways are peppered with unique independent shops.

LEFT: Tourists and locals shopping and walking at the bustling Hongdae street market at night.

ABOVE: Spring cherry blossom at Changdeokgung Palace in Seoul.

Itaewon

It's no secret that this neighbourhood once had a seedy reputation as a hub for prostitution houses entertaining American soldiers at the nearby US military base. But after 9/11, soldiers were placed on strict curfew lockdown and those seedy bars closed down, replaced by the many foreign restaurants and cafes you see today. Considering itself a 'multicultural Gangnam', the area is full of foreign business owners catering to tourists as well as locals.

The area has a free-spirited, bohemian feel because of its foreign population, which is different from the traditionally conservative outlook of Koreans from older generations. Among Itaewon's unique streets is Gyeongnidan, which offers an eclectic choice of international food from China, Thailand, Greece, India, Italy, France and more. The Usadan is another street worth exploring for its juxtaposition of the old and new, with trendy artists breathing new life into its old buildings from the 1960s.

The neighbourhood also hosts the Itaewon Global Village Festival, celebrating its multicultural identity, every year in October.

When in Seoul ...

With so much to see in this dynamic city, here are just a few of many attractions you may come across.

Natural wonders: there are several hiking trails along the city's surrounding mountains, including the spectacular Mt. Namsan, where you can stop by the N Seoul Tower for 360-degree panoramic views of the cityscape from its top-floor revolving restaurant.

Walkers can also explore trails along the Seoul City Wall, which was built during the Joseon Dynasty to protect the capital from invaders. The trails traverse the edges of all four mountains that enclose the capital, including Naksan, Bukaksan, Inwangsan and Namsan, offering spectacular views over the capital.

For more nature in the city, stroll down the Cheonggyecheon, a stream stretching from the Cheonggye Plaza outside the Gwanghwamun (the main gate of the Gyeongbokgung Palace) to Yangnyeong Market where it eventually merges with the Han River. This historic natural stream from the Joseon Dynasty remained buried under an overpass until 2005 when the site was restored and transformed into a scenic public walkway.

Landmarks: the city houses five UNESCO World Heritage Sites, which include the Changdeokgung Palace (one of the capital's historic Five Grand Palaces), the Hwaseong Fortress, the Jongmyo Shrine, Namhansanseong (a mountainous area just outside Seoul that served as an emergency capital for administrative and military functions during the Joseon period) and the Royal Tombs of the Joseon Dynasty.

Markets and shops: a trip to Gwangjang Market is a must for its street food galore, from *kimbap* (seaweed wrap rice rolls) and *dukbokgi* (spicy rice cakes) to *haemul pajeon* (seafood pancakes).

The historic Namdaemun Market, which has been around for more than 600 years, offers a hodgepodge of everything you could possibly need, from cheap clothes to home goods and beyond.

The Dongdaemun area, where Seoul Fashion Week takes place every year, is the city's fashion hub and Dongdaemun Market offers a variety of clothing stalls, featuring both modern and vintage styles.

Myeongdong is another main shopping area good for affordable prices, with a wide selection of Korean cosmetic shops and large retailers such as Lotte Department Store, Shinsegae Department Store and the Myeongdong Migliore, as well as global brands from Zara to H&M.

Insadong is a historic neighbourhood where painters used to study during the Joseon Dynasty. Today, it is the place to go for Korean antiques, crafts and other local artwork and traditional items unique to the country.

Hanok **villages:** these preserved historic villages are found in pockets of Korea, such as in Bukchon and Seochon in Seoul. The homes in these villages were once the residence of the nobility during the Joseon Dynasty era but today have been restructured and restored to serve as cafes, restaurants, workshops, guesthouses for tourists and other places offering cultural experiences.

These well-preserved homes have retained much of their traditional features including rooms with *ondol bangs* (underfloor heating). Elsewhere in the country, *hanok* villages can be found in Andong, Gyeongju and Jeonju.

RIGHT: Two women wearing *hanbok* walking among the traditional style houses of Bukchon *hanok* village.

Busan

Growing up my impression of Busan was that of an old-fashioned 'country bumpkin' scene, based on the distinct southern drawl you'll hear among locals, which is similar to the accent of my dad's family from the Gyeongsangbukdo province, just north of the Gyeongsangnamdo province adjacent to Busan.

But today South Korea's second city, with a population of around 3.5 million, is a thriving urban hub in its own right, full of glamorous locals living it up on some of the priciest plots of land outside Seoul. The former capital of Gyeongsangnamdo even launched its own local currency in 2019 known as the *Dongbaekjeon*, a blockchain-based local currency card, to further boost its already

booming economy. The currency can be used at participating shops, department stores and other local venues, with users said to be rewarded a six percent cashback payout per transaction.

Busan easily rivals Seoul with equally buzzy patches of cultural activity (with the added bonus of a nearby beach coast to retire to when in need of a break), from mouth-watering street-food stalls to landmarks such as the historic Gamcheon Cultural Village, a collection of brightly painted houses dotted along steep twisting alleyways that are peppered with various colourful works of local art. It's been locally dubbed the 'Machu Picchu of Busan' for its steep mountain-side location.

The fifth busiest port in the world, Busan hosts Asia's top international film festival – the Busan International Film Festival –

ABOVE: **View overlooking Gamcheon Cultural Village with Busan harbour in the distance.**

ABOVE: The Lotus Lantern Festival in Samgwangsa Temple, Busan, May 2018.

and other cultural events such as the Lotus Lantern Festival, which celebrates the birth of Buddha with the release of thousands of colourful lanterns during this time, especially at the Samgwangsa Temple. This Buddhist temple is of the Cheontae Order, one of Korea's mainstream Buddhist denominations, and its 30m-high Dabotap Tower is said to be the largest stone pagoda in all of Asia. The Busan Fireworks Festival is one of the country's largest firework events, attracting more than a million visitors every autumn and featuring a high-tech laser light show.

Some of the country's most popular beaches are in Busan, such as Haeundae and Gwangalli, which are lined with several luxury hotels, complexes and other high rises, as well as three historic markets. They include the Gukje Market, which was featured in the film *Ode to My Father* (a 2014 South Korean historical film charting Korea's history from the 1950s to the present day that became one of the highest-grossing films in Korean cinema history) and the Bupyeong Khangtong Market. Here you can sample some of the best local foods that Busan is known for, including *bokguk* (blowfish soup), *bibim dangmyeon* (spicy sweet and sour glass noodles) and *Busan eomuk* (Busan fish cakes).

Busan's Centum City shopping centre was once the world's largest department store back in 2009, surpassing even the Macy's department store in New York City in the Guinness Book of World Records.

When in Busan ...

Busan Cinema Centre: the official venue of the Busan International Film Festival (BIFF), which takes place in October every year attracting Korean and international celebrities from around the world, features various arthouse cinema and other performances from musicals to theatre shows and more. The complex also features one of the world's largest LED roofs with a wave-like shape. It was the world's longest cantilevered roof at the time it was built back in 2012.

The success of the film festival is charted around BIFF Plaza where several Korean celebrities, as well as global film stars such as Jeremy Irons, have left handprints (much like at Grauman's Chinese Theatre on the historic Hollywood Walk of Fame) and several celebrities can be seen hanging out in the local cafes, restaurants and hotels during the festival itself.

Markets: Bupyeong Khangtong Market is a feast for the senses, with alley after alley of food stalls selling some of the most iconic Korean street food, as well as unique local delicacies and other exotic Asian foods from parts of Southeast Asia such as Vietnam. The historic market dates back to 1945 and is the country's first night market, opening around 7pm each night.

The market was formerly a place that sold only foreign goods – mostly canned food obtained from the US military, hence its name *khangtong*, which means 'tin can' in Korean. But today, it's known for its street food stalls and sells a variety of goods, from electronics and appliances to clothing and vintage items at bargain prices.

Gukje Market, a similar type of venue, opened a few years later, around the 1950s, just after the Korean War with the same premise (*gukje* means 'foreign' in Korean). Both markets, as well as the Jagalchi Market, are connected and accessible from the Jagalchi train station, so they can be explored on the same visit.

ABOVE: Clear blue skies at popular Gwangalli Beach. BELOW Decorative detail at Beomeosa Temple.

Beaches: Busan's coast is set against a backdrop of skyscrapers, flanked by several high rises, including luxury hotels as well as the city's high-end restaurants, bars and cafes. Two of South Korea's most popular beaches are in Busan – Haeundae Beach and Gwangalli Beach.

Haeundae is South Korea's largest beach, and has been featured in several of Korea's biggest television drama series. The district of the same name in which the beach sits is the most expensive area outside the Seoul Capital Area, and is home to some of the country's wealthiest citizens, as well as major skyscrapers such as the 'Haeundae Doosan We've the Zenith' tower, among various others in development.

Gwangalli Beach, with its half-moon, crescent-shaped coast, is popular for its fine sand and trendy restaurants, bars and clubs along the shoreline, and hugs the length of the Gwangandaegyo Bridge, the city's famed suspension bridge, which sits against a backdrop of high-rise towers. The beach as well as the bridge and Jagalchi Market were featured in a car chase scene in the 2018 Hollywood Blockbuster film *Black Panther*. Gwangalli Beach is also near the Busan Yachting Centre, where the yachting competitions for the 1988 Olympics were held.

Temples: Busan houses incredible historic temples such as the Beomeosa Temple, which was built in 678 during the Silla Kingdom and has been registered among Korea's official National Treasures. Most of it was destroyed following Japanese invasions in 1502 but restoration works have been ongoing since 1602. It's known today for its autumn foliage and lush greenery during the spring.

The Haedong Yonggungsa Temple, dating back to 1376, is among the few seaside temples in Korea, set on a cliff overlooking the coast in northern Busan. It's especially popular for its cherry blossoms in April and sunrise views on New Year's Day. The Samgwangsa Temple also offers spectacular cityscape views year-round and is open 24 hours a day.

Jeju island

Dubbed as Korea's version of Hawaii, Jejudo (Jeju Island) is a paradise of pristine beaches, lush forests, spectacular waterfalls and an otherworldly volcanic landscape, which formed nearly 2 million years ago.

In recent years, the self-governing province has been on the radar of foreign tourists but among locals it's traditionally been a honeymoon destination and still is, among many loved-up couples. There's even a very tongue-in-cheek, erotically themed park called Love Land on the island, which perhaps plays an exaggerated homage to its tradition as the ultimate honeymoon island.

Jejudo is a key beach destination for locals in South Korea and residents of other Asian countries nearby, because of its subtropical climate, with cool and dry winters as well as hot, humid and, at times, rainy summers.

While tourism is the main source of the local economy and contributes to the country's larger economy, the island is protective of its unspoilt landscape.

RIGHT: People enjoying the white sand and clear waters of Jeju Island.

When in Jejudo …

Natural wonders: the province is home to three UNESCO World Heritage sites. One is the island's extensive system of lava caves, with multicoloured roofs, floors and dark walls covered by a mural of carbonate deposits, through which lava once flowed. It's known as one of the largest lava-tube cave systems in the world with unique formations and other features.

Forming the centre of the volcanic terrain, the UNESCO-designated Hallasan is South Korea's highest mountain. Housing more plant species than any other single mountain in the world (around 1,562 plants), half of Korea's plant species are naturally found on Hallasan and the island's flora uniquely spans three zones – the subtropic, temperate and frigid zones. Its lake-filled crater forms the summit of the mountain, and is part of Hallasan National Park, a virtually untouched forested landscape with unique cliffs, rock formations, waterfalls and hiking paths.

The dramatic Seongsan Ilchulbong tuff cone, which rises out of the ocean resembling the shape of a fortress, forms the island's third UNESCO site.

A unique clan of female divers on the island known as *haenyeo* are also UNESCO-designated as Intangible Cultural heritage. It's one of the only examples of a matriarchal structure in all of Korea, where females were the head of the household providing the primary source of income through this diving work. The diving tradition on Jeju dates back to 434 AD and the first recorded evidence of it was in the 17th century. By the 18th century, the *haenyeo* had outnumbered the male divers in the community.

LEFT: The Seongsan Ilchulbong peak in the summer on Jeju Island.

Beaches: dive into the cobalt blue waters of Jungmun Saekdal Beach, which has been the backdrop of various Korean films and television dramas, with its striking black basalt rocks and multi-coloured sand.

For a classic white-sand beach caressed by picturesque emerald-green waves, Hyeopjae Beach will do just fine. The 9-kilometre beach is surrounded by an evergreen forest, where visitors can also enjoy camping by the beach.

Evidence of the island's volcanic history can be traced at the Daepo Jusangjeolli Cliff on the southern coast of Jeju Island, a cluster of hexagonal pillars that formed when Hallasan erupted. Similar in appearance to Giant's Causeway in Northern Ireland, the unique volcanic rock formation has been weathered by crashing ocean waves for thousands of years.

Cape Seopjikoji, made from red volcanic ash called *songi*, on the east coast is another volcanic vantage point best enjoyed in the spring when the rapeseed flowers are in bloom.

More coastal scenes can be had on the Aewol-Hagwi coastal drive, one of the island's famous scenic coastal roads, which leads to the island's most beautiful beaches including Gwakchi and Geumneung, in addition to Hyeopjae.

Gardens: tucked away in the western pockets of the island are manicured botanical and bonsai gardens of wild flowers at Hallim Park, while the Yeomiji Botanical Garden houses around 2,000 rare plants including ones native to the island.

Forest trails: the island has one of the largest single species of forest in the world at Bijarim Forest, which has nearly 3,000 trees aged between 500 and 800 years, including a 14-metre-tall 'grandfather' tree believed to be around 820 years old.

The Hwansang Forest in the southwest region houses rich, well-preserved eco systems that are unique to Jejudo, while the Saryeoni Forest Trail is known as the 'healing forest' with its abundance of phytoncide emitted by various cypress, cedar and oak trees along its 15-km trail.

PREVIOUS PAGE: **The peak of South Korea's highest mountain, Mt. Hallasan, shrouded in morning fog.**

Island escapes: go island hopping around the smaller islands of Jejudo, including to Biango Island, which is visible from Hyeopjae Beach. It's said that the island can be fully explored on foot in about two hours, or half a day for some. It can be reached by ferry service from Hallim Park.

Udo Island, off the east coast of Jejudo, is home to Seobin Baeksa, another white-sand beach that's one of the most popular tourist spots in Jejudo, while the uninhabited Munseom Island is a treat for divers for its rich coral colonies, with the sun reaching 40 metres deep in the waters.

On Marado Island, visitors can walk to the southernmost point of South Korea and see unusually shaped rock formations, dramatic cliff faces and the Cheonyeodang Shrine, which is dedicated to prayer for the safety of the female divers on the island.

Other unmissable hotspots

Each of South Korea's diverse regions offers a unique glimpse and taste of the country's cultural landscape. Here are some of the key cities and provinces worth exploring to uncover the country's eclectic culture and heritage.

Incheon

Sitting just outside Seoul, Incheon is South Korea's third largest city. It houses Incheon Airport, the main international hub of the country, which has been named among the world's best airports for several consecutive years due to its high-tech facilities. The city's Bupyeong Station is where the Seoul subway and Incheon subway intersect. But the station is also known for its network of underground shops (mostly selling women's clothes and mobile phones) where there are 1,408 stores spanning across 31,692m (according to stats from the National Archives of Korea). In 2014, it was officially certified as having the largest number of stores in the world by the American World Record Academy. Above the station there are other shopping areas, such as the Lotte Mart, and several restaurants.

Daegu

This up-and-coming city in the Gyeongsangbukdo province is a place where tradition meets innovation, with some of the country's oldest markets standing next to modern shopping complexes and performance art centres. Its historic textile business has been coming into its own in recent years, with a burgeoning fashion industry in the city. Dongseongro is similar to Seoul's Myeongdong, where you'll find the best fashion shops. Daegu is also home to the country's oldest medicinal herb market dating back nearly 360 years. It's a wholesale market and is the main distribution centre for medicinal herbs across the country.

LEFT: Whale figures in the central park of Songdo International Business District in Incheon.

ABOVE: **Seoraksan National Park in Gangwondo.**

Gangwondo

This historic province, one of the original eight provinces of the Joseon Dynasty, is bordered in the north by the Military Demarcation Line (MDL), which marks the land border with North Korea within the southern half of the Demilitarized Zone (DMZ). The northern half of the province sits in North Korea's portion of the DMZ.

This area is popular among foreign tourists wanting to absorb the complex history of the peninsula, especially the Joint Security Area (JSA), an area where North and South Korean soldiers come face to face while standing guard.

The JSA features several conference rooms, which the MDL also bisects, where political officials from both sides of the border come together for meetings. Visitors are able to see these rooms and even cross over to the other side within them. The JSA is just one of the DMZ sites that can be explored in the area. Others include Freedom Bridge, Infiltration Tunnels, Odusan Unification Observatory, Dora Observatory and Nuri Peace Park.

While there is plenty of history to be absorbed in Gangwondo, around 77 percent of the region is mountainous, making it a popular country escape for locals. The province is home to four national parks within the Taebaek Mountains, which stretch across both North and South Korea, along the eastern edge of the peninsula. Mount Taebaeksan forms Taebaek National Park.

The other national parks include Seoraksan National Park, one of the most popular holiday destinations among Korean locals. Seoraksan is listed in UNESCO's Man and the Biosphere Programme, which is dedicated to the further study of biodiversity loss, sustainability and climate change in selected biosphere reserves around the world.

Gangwondo is also home to Pyeongchang, which is popular for skiing breaks at its two main ski resorts Yongpyong and Alpensia, both of which were used in the 2018 Winter Olympics.

Gangwondo boasts beautiful coastal stretches including Gyeongpo Beach, the largest beach on the eastern coast known for its soft, powdery sand and Sokcho Beach, a white-sand stretch that is one of the country's most popular beaches.

Gyeongju

The Gyeongsangbukdo province is known as the birthplace of Korea's cultural traditions and Confucian culture, from which many of the Korean customs and traditional beliefs have emerged. Gyeongju, the province's second city, heralds a history of more than 1,000 years dating back to the Silla Kingdom when it served as the capital of the kingdom.

The city features several UNESCO sites, including the Seokguram grotto/shrine (in its main chamber there is a large Buddha statue seated cross-legged on a lotus throne) and Bulguksa Temple – both of which form part of the Bulguksa Temple complex – as well as the Gyeongju Historic Areas and Yangdong Folk Village, located just 16km outside Gyeongju.

The Seokguram grotto and Bulguksa Temple were the first Korean sites to ever be included in a UNESCO listing when they received their designation in

1995. Bulguksa Temple is lauded as the grand masterpiece from the golden age of Buddhism during the Silla era. It is among the head temples of the Jogye Order, which is the main order representing Korean Buddhism.

Andong

The capital of the Gyeongsangbukdo province is considered 'Korea's spiritual capital'. Once known as the centre for Confucian academies during the Joseon Dynasty, Andong was where many *yangban* (Korean aristocrats who became scholars) resided and studied during the era.

The city is known for maintaining ancient traditions and folk culture, such as the *hahoetal*, which are unique traditional masks that depict different characters featured in the *byeolsin-gut*, ritual masked dance dramas and a shamanist rite honouring the communal spirits of the village. Dating back to around the 12th century, the dance ceremony has been named an intangible cultural asset by the country, while the masks have been named among South Korea's officially designated National Treasures. Andong's

ABOVE: Traditional wooden masks in Andong.

UNESCO-designated Hahoe Folk Village site is known for *byeolsin-gut*. The city's ancient culture is celebrated during the Andong Folk Festival every year.

Back in 1999, Her Majesty, Queen Elizabeth II of the UK visited Andong, spending her 73rd birthday in the city.

Jeollado

The Jeolla region (made up of the Jeollanamdo and Jeollabukdo provinces) sits on the southwest coast of the country. The area is known for its rich regional cuisine, showcasing local delicacies including seafood such as oysters and seaweed. The region still uses the same ingredients that are believed to have been consumed by wealthy nobles who lived in the area during the era of the Joseon Dynasty.

Jeollanamdo is home to the metropolitan city of Gwangju, the province's largest city (and the country's sixth largest overall), which hosts the Gwangju Biennale. This contemporary art festival has been running September–November every two to three years from 1995, and is now among the top five biggest biennales in the world.

Food lovers can take a food tour of the region, sampling various dishes for which each city is known, such as the Jeonju *bibimbap*, a regional version

ABOVE: Octopus stall in Gyeongju market.

ABOVE: Gunsan speciality seafood noodle dish, *jjamppong*.
BELOW: 18-metre Buddha statue at Gwanchoksa Temple.

of the classic mix-rice dish served in a hot-stone bowl, mixed with spicy red pepper paste and topped with a raw egg. In Jeonju, the provincial capital of Jeollabukdo, this dish is served with *yookhweh* (basically beef tartare).

Elsewhere, there is the Gunsan *jjamppong*. This is a spicy seafood noodle dish found across the country but is among the city of Gunsan's specialities.

Chungcheongnamdo

Surrounded by large lakes and mountains, this province is ideal for a country escape and is a popular holiday destination for locals. It is also very easy to get to, given it is the only province outside the Seoul Capital Area served by Seoul's metro system.

Visitors will want to explore the country's historic attractions, including temples such as the Gwanchoksa, where you'll find the largest Buddha stone in the country, or Mount Gyeryong for its striking rock formations or one of its beaches including Daecheon Beach, the largest beach on the west coast of the country. The beach is known for its two grades of sand, which ranges from soft sand formed from eroded seashells found on the upper shores to the hard, packed sand closer to the shorelines, which is great for scrubs and skin health.

The other famous beach in the province is Muchangpo Beach, known for its beautiful, pine tree-lined coastal drives and sunsets, as well as a natural phenomenon known as the 'Moses Miracle' where extreme tides unveil the seabed for a short period of time two or three times a month. This exposed sea floor forms a 1.5-km path from the beach to Seokdaedo island. This phenomenon, which happens around the 15th and 30th August/September, is celebrated at the Muchangpo Mystic Sea Road Festival every year.

North Korea

According to legend, the ancient kingdom of Gojoseon was established around 2333 BC, developed by a refugee from China who founded a colony in Pyongyang in what is North Korea today. The kingdom saw further Chinese invasions around 300 BC before it collapsed in the second century BC. Pyongyang was the capital of the Gojoseon and Koguryŏ (37 BC to 668 AD) kingdoms and was the secondary capital of the Koryŏ Dynasty. It serves as North Korea's capital today.

Most of the country's population of around 25.5 million is concentrated in the plains and lowlands found in the western provinces – mostly around Pyongyang, the district of Hungnam in Hamhung (the third largest city in North Korea), as well as the city of Wonsan. The country is slightly larger in area than South Korea, which spans approximately 100,360sq km, while North Korea covers around 123,138sq km. Nearly 80 percent of its terrain is covered by mountains, the highest of which is Mount Baekdu at 2,750m.

Often described as the world's most secretive nation, it's no surprise that travellers are curious to explore North Korea – one of the few Communist states in the world. Most people get a glimpse of the country from the South Korean side of the border at the DMZ. But adventurous travellers can get a closer look from the Northern side as well. Tourism exists in the country on a limited basis and visits can only be done as part of a group tour led by the state-funded Korea International Travel Company, in collaboration with a handful of local tour operators such as Regent Holidays in England, Koryo Tours in Beijing, China and several others in Europe and Asia.

If you do overcome the difficulties in visiting, North Korea is home to historic sites such as the UNESCO-designated Koguryŏ tombs, a complex of tombs from the kingdom of the same name believed to have been the burial sites of kings and queens from that era. They are located in the cities of Pyongyang and Nampo. Overall, there are more than 10,000 tombs from the ancient Koguryŏ kingdom left in existence and are the only remains of this ancient culture. Only around 90 of them have wall paintings, which depict what everyday life was like during the Koguryŏ era. These vibrant murals are considered masterpieces from the Koguryŏ Dynasty and demonstrate the engineering capabilities of the period, while offering insight on daily life and burial customs of that era.

RIGHT: **Statues of former North Korean Presidents Kim Il Sung and Kim Jong Il on Mansu Hill, Pyongyang.**

ABOVE: Cherry blossom on display in South Korea.

When to visit

South Korea generally has a temperate climate and four distinct seasons, with a terrain of mostly hills and mountains and 2,413km of coast. Around 70 percent of the country is mountainous, with the highest mountain being Hallasan.

Rainfall tends to be heavy in the summer, as are the temperatures and humidity. The country basically has the opposite of a Mediterranean climate. Due to the Asian monsoon cycle, the driest periods are during the winter, while the rainiest season is the summer.

Winters in the interior and the north can be brutally cold and ever so mildly warmer along the southern coast. The winters are so cold because of the wind coming down from Siberia. Seoul, which is located along the coast but in the north-west, is the area most exposed to cold winds, while cities along the southern coast like Busan have milder temperatures.

With winters being extremely cold and the height of the summers being pretty hot, the best times to visit are autumn and spring, naturally for their more pleasant temperatures. High season for travel is the summer due to local families travelling around the country on holiday when the school term is done.

Spring is the season for viewing the beautiful cherry blossom, which usually blooms from around March to mid-April. Cherry blossoms can be seen most visibly in the Five Grand Palaces of Seoul, which really make you feel like you're in another time period, surrounded by such traditional flowers against a backdrop of ancient quarters and architecture.

Getting around

South Korea's transportation network was vastly developed during the first decade after the country was first established. By 1968, the country built its first multi-lane motorway from Seoul to Incheon and created an expanded express highway system that allowed easier transport between major cities across the country. At this time, there were more automobiles in the country due to the thriving auto industry and travel by car became prevalent, while a domestic air travel service was also introduced in this period.

Planes: there are two major international airports, the most frequented being Incheon International, which has been named the world's best airport by Skytrax

for several consecutive years, noted for its high-tech facilities. Gimpo Airport used to be the main international hub, before Incheon airport was unveiled in 2001, and now serves only domestic destinations. The AREX railway connects you to Gimpo or Incheon from Seoul. There are also several other international airports in South Korea, including in Busan and Jejudo.

Metro: Seoul's underground metro system was expanded in the 1990s and it is the easiest and most efficient way of getting around town. It features several different lines that cut through the city, with spacious, high-tech carriages with Wi-Fi, and is well-signposted in terms of the station names and super easy to follow. You can buy City Pass cards (T Money and Mpass – metropolitan pass – cards for foreigners) or other multi-day travel cards that offer value for money.

Trains: the construction of high-speed trains from the 1990s has helped dramatically cut travel time across the country, such as between Seoul and Busan, which now takes just over 2.5 hours to do by high-speed railway, rather than the previous more than four hours.

It's easy to get around to explore different parts of the country by train using a pass card. Back in 2018, the KTX company launched a new high-speed train between Pyeongchang and Seoul for the Winter Olympics. High-speed train allows easy travel between the airport and the city centre of Seoul and other cities. KORAIL pass is a handy travel card to have for train journeys.

Buses: the country's bus network is well-organised and is one of the cheapest ways of getting around, but it requires a bit more local knowledge to navigate. Travellers can use the T Money and Mpass cards on buses. There are also express and intercity express buses available for travel across cities, in addition to local buses for which you can pay by cash or transportation card.

Taxis: available 24 hours a day, taxi journeys can be paid for in cash or using a T Money card or credit card. The Korea Travel Hotline can be used for any interpretation assistance by dialing 1330 from any phone.

LEFT: A sculptural structure that plays media art in the duty-free shopping area at Incheon International Airport.

The Korean
Spirit

Family life, Korean style

It's hard to find a culture where family isn't important in some way, shape or form. It's a universal thread that runs through the fabric of life across all boundaries and what brings people together in all corners of the world.

In Korean society, family is not simply important – it's everything. Family forms the bedrock from which the foundation of its culture has been built and from where key aspects of its cultural beliefs and norms radiate. There may be no other group where the saying 'Blood is thicker than water' rings more true than among Koreans.

Traditional Korean parents see it as their duty to do anything and everything for their children. But with this sacrifice comes an unspoken expectation that their children will do the same for them when they are grown up. With the exception of some modern families, the notion of parents devoting their entire lives to their children so that the children will also look after their parents is still an underlying principle within Korean family structure. It's why it's not unusual for Koreans to live with their parents through adulthood until they get married, even after which some remain living with either their parents or in-laws.

This sense of unconditional devotion, honour and duty towards family can be traced back to the country's background in Confucian beliefs, which thrived especially during the Joseon Dynasty. Filial piety was one of the classic Confucian teachings and looking after your family, especially your parents and other elder members, and honouring them after their passing in the form of ancestral worship was practised by the kings and queens of the Koryŏ and Joseon Dynasties.

Evidence of this historic devotion to family can be seen at the UNESCO-designated Royal Tombs of the Joseon Dynasty, a collection of 40 tombs of former kings and queens carefully curated throughout 18 locations on the peninsula, and the UNESCO-designated Jongmyo Shrine in Seoul, which is the oldest and most authentic royal ancestral Confucian shrine in the world. It was frequented by kings during the Joseon era to pray for the safety of the country through ancestral worship ceremonies, which are still carried out today every year to honour the late kings and queens. While the roots of these ceremonies are based on Confucian beliefs, rituals of honouring ancestors are practised among nearly all Korean families today, regardless of their creed and are adapted according to their religious beliefs.

RIGHT: South Koreans perform a ritual for the deceased kings of the Joseon Dynasty at the royal shrine of Jongmyo.

The importance of education

Education has been viewed as the key to success in life among Koreans from as early as the dynasty eras when it was the only way to gain wealth and power in society. Unlike aristocracies in European societies, nobility status in Korea was not granted based on family lineage alone. During the Joseon Dynasty, to become a *yangban* (an aristocrat), one had to pass the aforementioned *gwageo* (national civil service examination), which required years of studying the Confucian classics and history, not just once but several times. Therefore, *yangbans* were considered scholars in society because of the many years of study and exams they had to undergo to achieve their title. As a result, most *yangbans* tended to be appointed in positions of power such as in government or within the military.

While technically any member of society, regardless of class, could attempt to gain *yangban* status, realistically it was only the wealthy and the children of *yangban* families who had the financial means to pursue the education required to pass the *gwageo*. But it was also said that *yangban* families who did not produce another *yangban* within three generations could lose their noble title and be demoted to commoner status. So in some ways, success was viewed not only as requiring hard work, but also as fragile and a status that you needed to work hard to maintain.

This link between education and success remains a strong driving force in Korean culture today. Exams continue to play an important role as a pathway to a better education, a better career and the upper echelons of society.

It's not uncommon to see parents praying at temples or churches on the day of national exams in a plea for the educational success of their child, which to them ultimately means success in their own lives, knowing that not only will they be taken care of but their children will be able to look after themselves after they have passed away.

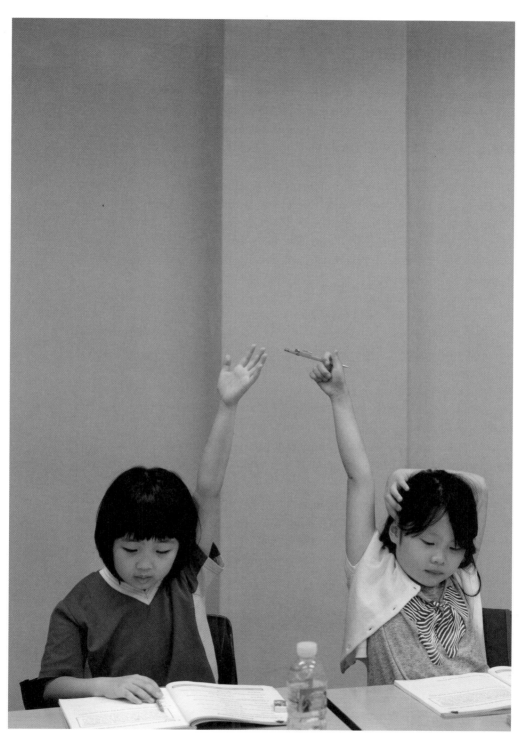

ABOVE: Pupils at the Jongno Hagwon Academy in Mok-dong area of Seoul.

Given Korea's history as a poor nation, many of the older generations grew up in poverty, so they cling to this vision of education leading to a stable job and equating to financial security. And stable jobs seem to fall into one of two categories to most Korean parents – either a doctor or a lawyer.

Locals say (half-jokingly) that a Korean mother hopes to have 'three sets of keys' given to her from her son (or daughter) when her children grow up – one set of keys to their own house, another for their own car and another for their 'officetel' (a studio apartment), as a picture of their success. Officetels (a combination of the words 'office' and 'hotel') serve as a living/work space for professionals and are common in urban cities in South Korea.

While many families of younger generations have evolved following the influence of Western culture in recent years, this somewhat singular view of the pathway to success remains a latent part of the DNA of Korean society.

The first step to educational success: Schooling

Compulsory education in South Korea entails six years in primary school followed by three years in middle school, both of which are provided for free nationally. Students are assigned to schools according to their residential district at these levels.

High-school education lasts for three years and is not provided free. But options are more varied, ranging from general academic high schools, specialised schools for specific subjects and private, elite high schools (which are more expensive) to vocational high schools that provide training in specific trades for those who opt to skip university.

The average school day for high-school students begins around 8.00 a.m. and lasts until 4.00 or 4.30 p.m., with a lunch break of about 50 minutes. The classes are each about 50 minutes long and the teachers move from room to room, while the students remain in the same classroom throughout the day.

Studies continue after school at either the school library or commonly at *hagwons*, which are after-school prep academies that provide extra tutoring. High-school students are often at *hagwons* until anywhere from 10.00 p.m. to midnight, clocking in nearly 12 to 16 hours of studying per day on average.

South Korea's students have been reported to study more hours than children in any other OECD country, while the country is said to have the biggest private tutoring industry in the world.

According to a 2014 survey by the country's National Youth Policy Institute, around 53 percent of the nearly 10,000 elementary and high-school students surveyed were found to have been sleep-deprived because of their studies. And 90 percent of those surveyed were reported to have less than two hours of free time on a weekday. This unhealthy level of dedication to studies has pushed the government to impose curfews on *hagwons* during the 2000s, limiting opening times to around 10.00 p.m.

High-school students in their third year – referred to as *goh sahm*, a shortened moniker for *gohdunghakgyo sahmhaknyeon*, which means 'third year of high school' in Korean – are especially under intense pressure to study rigorously in order to pass the required entrance exams for the country's top-ranking schools among the dozen or so national universities available.

These students often receive additional private tutoring outside normal school hours to help prepare for the university entrance exams. However, university admission does not solely depend on entrance exams, with several of the most elite schools looking at other criteria including students' scores within different subject areas, as well as extracurricular activities. But nonetheless, many schools place a big emphasis on these entrance exam scores.

But, as it was throughout history, those who have access to extra tutoring, and ultimately better access to higher education, are the wealthy upper-class members of society. Less than half of those who receive high-school education reportedly get a chance to attend university.

The latest administration under South Korea's current president Moon Jae In has proposed several measures of educational reform in a bid to even out the competition and allow financially disadvantaged students to have an equal chance of making it into university. Some of these moves have included a reduction in admission fees and the easing of the exam difficulty levels in order to eliminate the need for extra tutoring to pass the exams.

NEXT PAGE: Parents pray at Chogey temple in Seoul for success for their children taking examinations.

Continuing the good work: Further Education

Providing an international education overseas has been another way that Korean parents have attempted to give their children an edge in the competitive labour market.

The popularity for studies abroad grew in the late 20th and 21st centuries, especially in the US where it peaked in 2011 with around 129,000 students enrolled. Many Koreans have traditionally sought an American education for the world-ranking status of top US universities, as well as to perfect their English and ultimately increase their job prospects in Korea.

As of 2017, 57 percent of Korean students abroad were studying in the US, followed by 12 percent in Japan, 6 percent in Australia, 5 percent in the UK and 4.5 percent in Canada, according to the UNESCO Institute for Statistics. Other popular destinations included France, Malaysia, New Zealand and Italy.

China has also become a growing hotspot for overseas studies among Koreans, since around 2013, in order to learn Mandarin, which has been an advantage in the Korean job market, given the important trade relations between both countries.

But foreign education has also provided less of an advantage in the job market in recent years, with more employers in South Korea seeking employees who are better-connected domestically in terms of contacts and background.

ABOVE: Studying at Starfield Public Library in Seoul.

Koreans at work

The idea of undying duty and unconditional loyalty towards your family can also be seen in the work life of Korean society at a subtle level across different sectors. The head of a company and other company superiors are to be respected in the way you would respect the head of a family household.

The top-ranking officials of a company tend to enjoy all the perks and benefits, while others at a lower level are expected to work not only hard, but harder than others above their own level. These unspoken hierarchies established in the workplace are implicitly influenced by Confucian ethics, such as putting the importance of the needs of a group over that of an individual within a company. This idea has played out especially throughout the history of the *chaebols* (family-run conglomerates).

While Confucian principles might have previously relegated women to lower positions in the social hierarchy, the modern age has seen a reduction in this narrow view of women, even among *chaebol* groups like Samsung, whose chairman Lee Kun Hee implemented several measures to promote equality for women. Back in 1994, company executives were ordered by Lee to pay and treat men and women at the company equally. He also banned female uniforms and required at least 20 percent of new employees to be female, as well as built several child-care centres at company premises to assist working moms at Samsung.

As of 2019, women reportedly only account for around 3.6 percent of the top executive positions at the country's 100 biggest corporations, according to a survey by South Korean recruitment consultancy Unico Search. Among those, Samsung Electronics was reported to have a slightly higher than average portion of female executives at 5 percent.

In terms of social norms at work, given a company is seen like an extended family, it's commonplace for colleagues to socialise and go for drinks or a meal after work. Drinking is a big part of Korean culture (more to come on this in a later chapter) and it's seen as a way of bonding in both work and personal settings.

Language

The Korean language was established in the 15th century by King Sejong during the Joseon Dynasty. Before then, Koreans used a language based on a version of Chinese characters, known as *hanja* (which is still taught in schools today), which were reserved for the elite in society. King Sejong wanted to provide a language that commoners could use, since they didn't have the access nor the time to learn the Chinese characters used by the upper classes.

He established the Korean language known today as *hangul* (한글), which is made of 10 vowels and 14 consonants. Korean is spoken in both the North and South of the peninsula. The basics are the same in terms of the use of the same alphabet, but the accent, as well as certain phrases, are different between North and South Koreans. There are also a few regional accents – known as *sahtooree* – that sound different across parts of South Korea, some of which can be difficult to understand if you're a non-native speaker.

The language reflects Koreans' emphasis on respect, making sure that due honour is given to the appropriate people in our interactions. There is a familiar tone and a formal tone for different words that need to be adjusted accordingly depending on the person you are speaking with. It would be considered a big faux pas to inappropriately use a familiar tone when speaking to a stranger or someone very elderly.

Here, I will explore some common phrases, proverbs and slang terms (spelled out phonetically in English in brackets) that you might come across among Korean locals.

Common phrases

수고하세요 (*su goh ha seh yo*): in the literal sense, this phrase translates to 'Continue to work hard', but it's the equivalent of saying 'Have a nice day'. You use it to say goodbye to someone working at a shop or other service venue but it can be used in any setting when saying goodbye (in a formal tone) to a person who is working.

잘 먹겠습니다 (*jal muk geht sup nee dah*): means 'I'll savour this food' and is said just before you tuck into a meal (served usually by elders) as a way of giving thanks to those who prepared the meal.

잘 먹었습니다 (*jal muk uht sup nee dah*): means 'I enjoyed the food' and is a way of giving thanks after a meal you've just consumed.

조심히 들어가세요 (*jo sheem ee deu ruh gah seh yo*): this literally reads 'Be careful as you go inside' but it's the equivalent of saying 'Have a safe journey home'. The phrase is used to say goodbye to someone in a formal tone.

두말하면 잔소리지 (*doo mal ha myun jan so ree gee*): the literal translation is 'Saying it twice is nagging' but, in short, it's a cheeky equivalent of saying 'You can say that again!' or 'Of course!' It's said when you are emphatically agreeing with what someone just said.

배부른 소리하네 (*beh boo roon soh ree hah neh*): this phrase translates to 'You sound like your stomach is full', meaning 'You sound like you are no longer hungry'. It's a phrase used to call out a person for sounding arrogant, full of themselves or ungrateful.

Proverbs

믿는 도끼에 발등 찍힌다 (*mit nun dohk kkee eh bal doong jjee keen dah*): literally translates as 'You can hurt your feet by the axe that you trusted', but the phrase is said when you feel betrayed by someone you trusted or never expected to be betrayed by.

하늘의 별 따기 (*hanul eh byul ddah gee*): translating to 'Plucking a star from the sky', the phrase is used to refer to a situation that is extremely difficult or impossible.

아니 땐 굴뚝에 연기 날까? (*ah nee dden gool ddook eh yun gee nal kkah?*): this proverb translates to 'Have you ever seen smoke come out of an unlit chimney?', meaning where there's an effect, there's always a cause.

등잔 밑이 어둡다 (*deung jang mit chi uh dupe da*): the phrase translates to 'It's dark right below the lantern', meaning sometimes we can miss the most obvious of places.

누워서 떡 먹기 (*noo uh suh dduck muck gee*): translating to 'Eating rice cakes while laying down', the phrase refers to any situations that are easy, similar to the meaning behind 'A piece of cake' in English.

원숭이도 나무에서 떨어진다 (*won soong ee doh nah moo eh suh dduh ruh gin dah*): meaning 'Even a monkey can fall from a tree', this proverb refers to how all people, even experts, are prone to mistakes.

Slang

화이팅 (*hwah ee ting*): this Korean-style phonetic pronunciation of the English word 'fighting' is used to wish people good luck or cheer them onwards.

대박이다 (*dae bahk ee dah*): this phrase is the equivalent of 'We hit the jackpot!' and is used in a situation when you've succeeded at something, seen a very successful outcome or something was extremely well done.

짱이다 (*jjang ee yah*): means 'Wow, you're the best!' or 'This is the best!' and is used when you really approve of someone, something, a place or even a situation.

쪽팔려 (*jjohk pal yuh*): this is a phrase to say 'How embarrassing!' and is used in situations when you feel embarrassed or your pride is hurt, or you feel put down by another person or a situation.

재수없다 (*jeh su up suh*): this is short for saying 'You're (or I'm or we're) so unlucky' and is used when you are faced with a stroke of bad luck or to describe a person or situation with disdain.

열받아 (*yul bah duh*): the phrase literally translates to 'I'm getting a fever' but is used to convey when you are extremely angry and feeling hot-headed (metaphorically).

How Koreans see themselves and others

Koreans generally take pride collectively as a nation, as well as feel loyalty towards and identify with their individual hometowns within various provinces and cities across the country. Given the importance of family in Korean culture, community is highly valued and bonds can be tight-knit within remote rural communities. But large urban areas also have pockets of communities and it is commonplace for neighbours to know each other by face, at the very least, and look after each other, especially the more elderly members of the local community.

With a large foreign population living in the capital, South Koreans have been very welcoming towards foreigners and foreign culture. But South Korean nationality is currently granted based on the nationality or ethnicity of one or both of your parents, rather than the place of birth. Back in 2005, a law proposed by the conservative Grand National Party to allow anyone born in South Korea, regardless of their parents' background, to become nationals was knocked down due to public opposition. This protective sentiment towards Korean blood by some is believed to stem from the country's history of being invaded by foreign countries. Among some of the older population, there is a residual sense of bitterness towards Japan for example, for the tragedies they witnessed during the period of Japanese occupation.

Within the peninsula, South Koreans see themselves as more progressive than North Koreans in terms of their lifestyle and thinking. But they don't necessarily have any animosity towards North Koreans in the modern age. There have been several defectors from North Korea who have been naturalised in the South and have been welcomed by the government and community throughout history. There are also families who have been torn apart for years since the border split, and for that reason many in the South continue to hope for a peaceful reunification of the peninsula for the sake of these separated families.

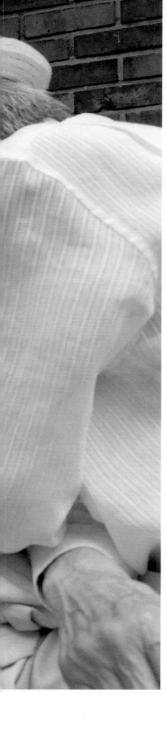

Ideology and respect for elders

Koreans are driven by respect and honour towards wisdom and knowledge. Education is held in such high measure because it leads to being respected and honoured in society, which Koreans believe translates to success in life. With family forming a core part of their value system, relationships are another main element of what drives Koreans' ideology and way of life. Knowing your place and how you fit into different circumstances are seen as the keys to navigating your way through life.

As children, Koreans are taught to have the utmost respect for all elders because they are deemed to have more life experience and therefore more wisdom than others. It doesn't matter if a person is older than you by a year or 50 years, you are expected to show the same respect to both. Respect is shown by the way an elder person is addressed in speech (a formal tone of phrase should be used when speaking) and in body language.

When you greet an elder person, you are normally expected to bend your upper body forward in a bowing motion out of respect. Speaking in an informal tone towards an elder person would be considered rude or accepting their handshake with just one of your own hands would also be seen as disrespectful. While some of these acts of respect might not be strictly observed between those who are only a few years or even months apart, the use of an informal tone of interaction would only be considered acceptable if the elder person permits it.

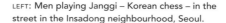

LEFT: Men playing Janggi – Korean chess – in the street in the Insadong neighbourhood, Seoul.

The art of nunchi

From a young age, my mum always said I seemed well-tuned into her moods and was keen to make her smile whenever I noticed she was feeling down. I remember standing beside her as she washed the dishes, popping my head from side to side in an attempt to catch her eye and pull cute faces to make her laugh away her bad feelings. I didn't know it at the time but this unassuming innocent act of care towards my mum was actually a natural display of quick *nunchi,* as my mum would say.

What exactly is nunchi?

The clue is in the word itself – the *nun* (pronounced 'noon') in *nunchi* means 'eyes' in Korean and *chi* means 'to measure'. So *nunchi* refers to looking around, to measure or assess your surroundings. It is the intuitive unspoken art of understanding the status quo of an environment, using a combination of gut feelings and all your senses.

In a modern age of health enthusiasts obsessed by self-awareness and mindfulness of the inner self, *nunchi* is an awareness of all things outward, including the external self and how you fit into the surrounding situation.

The power of nunchi

The purpose of *nunchi* is ultimately to promote harmony and peace in all circumstances. While there is no step-by-step, concrete formula for obtaining *nunchi* in the 'spark joy' type of way championed by Japanese author Marie Kondo, this guiding principle of awareness, when practised, can be useful in various areas of your life.

Having quick *nunchi* means being able to read a room, people and settings and act accordingly in the most appropriate or beneficial way possible to suit your needs, playing to the strengths and weaknesses of people and situations, which is a useful skill in all aspects of life.

Nunchi can be helpful in everyday settings such as at the market, where you might be looking to bag a bargain. Using *nunchi,* you can assess the mood of the seller to measure how likely it is that you might be able to get a price cut.

Or it comes into play in more personal circumstances, be it in relationships or friendships, when you might use *nunchi,* an inner gauge, to measure the tone of your interaction to determine what to say and when to say it.

The power of politics

The earliest introduction of South Korea's current government structure was during the Korean Provisional Government based in Shanghai in 1919, which followed a presidential system with three branches of power (legislative, administrative and judicial), modelled after the US government.

But the political climate of South Korea was turbulent for nearly 40 years following heavy-handed authoritarian rule over several presidential terms from 1948 through to the late 1980s. The first direct democratic election of a president in 16 years took place in 1987, with the election of Roh Tae Woo, who introduced measures of major government restructuring. The constitution

ABOVE: South Korea's National Assembly building in Seoul.

was revised in the same year and the government under the latest constitution has been known as The Six Republic since.

Since 1987, the president has been elected by popular vote for a single fixed five-year term, meaning the president cannot run for re-election. The National Assembly, consisting of 300 members elected every four years to represent various constituencies, holds legislative powers.

The voting age in South Korea was recently dropped from 19 to 18 years of age following a historic bill passed by The National Assembly in December 2019. In 2005, South Korea became the first country in Asia to allow foreigners who have lived in the country as permanent residents for three or more years to vote in local elections.

The president appoints the country's prime minister, which must be approved by The National Assembly. The president is the head of the state, government and serves as the commander of the armed forces, while The Supreme Court rules the judicial branch.

The country is run on a multi-party system but there have been several party splits and merges throughout history, which has also played a part in the fragility of the political landscape. There is more of an emphasis on individual politics rather than party loyalty, which has made political parties easily prone to splits following any form of disagreement.

South Korea's two main political parties today include the Democratic Party of Korea (the centrist liberal group and latest ruling party of The National Assembly) and the Liberal Korea Party (the conservative, far right-wing party).

The heavier political atmosphere of the past has seen many people, especially students, be very vocal in the form of passionate protests and has led to violent clashes with the police and government. However, the topic of politics on a day-to-day individual basis isn't necessarily a divisive subject in the modern age and generally South Koreans of today's generation are liberal, open-minded and accepting of differing views.

The spiritual question

South Korea does not have a national religion and freedom of religion is a constitutional right for all people. But several religions have shaped the country's social customs and cultural norms throughout history, such as the previously discussed Buddhism and Confucianism.

Shamanism, the belief in ancestral spirits, gods, demons and supernatural beings, has been around in the country since ancient times and is Korea's oldest indigenous religion. Many rituals related to Shamanism, such as ancestral worship and communicating with spirits through a priest or a shaman, are still practised by some in the country today.

Daoism, the Chinese philosophy around balance and harmony in life, is one of the earliest philosophies that shaped the peninsula. It was first brought to Korea around 624 AD by Emperor Gaozu, the founder of China's Tang Dynasty (618–907 AD), who sent priests to the peninsula with a book of ancient Chinese texts exemplifying Daoist principles. Daoism gained popularity and was practised in court rituals under King Yejong (the 16th king of the Koryŏ Dynasty) before its influence faded following the rise of Buddhism in the second half of the Koryŏ period. While Daoism remained dormant throughout the Joseon Dynasty, which was dominated by Confucianism, its importance in the history and culture of Korea today is signified on the South Korean flag. The blue and red circle at its centre, known as the *taegeuk*, symbolises the Daoist concept of yin and yang, representing the dualities in life and the balance achieved by the existence of two opposing forces, from good and evil to light and darkness and beyond.

Christianity was introduced towards the end of the 18th century, primarily through Roman Catholic missionaries, and has been a major factor in the modernisation of Korea. Today, about 25 percent of the country consider themselves Christians, most of whom are reported to be Protestants (either Presbyterian or Methodist), independent Christians or Roman Catholics. Less than a sixth of South Korea's population is said to be Buddhist, with nearly three million people reported to have abandoned the religion between 2005 and 2015. The drop in numbers could be down to several factors including the

RIGHT: Giant drum in the Buddhist temple of Bulguksa in Gyeongju.

ABOVE: Illuminated crosses displayed above a church in Seoul. BELOW LEFT: Lanterns in a South Korean temple. BELOW RIGHT: Buddha statue at Shinheungsa Buddhist temple, Seoraksan National Park.

modern age's lack of an urgent need for the basic material benefits (such as food, clothing, shelter) that the monastic life offers, which have become easily attainable by most in society. Buddhism's lack of community engagement and outreach due to the solitary and esoteric nature of its practices could also be contributing to its decline.

The majority of the country does not have a religion, while about a sixth are reported to be followers of new religions such as Taejongyo, which means 'Great Ancestral Worship', and Chondogyo, which translates to 'Teaching of the Heavenly Way' and is said to be a blend of Buddhist, Confucian, Christian and Daoist beliefs.

South Korean Flag

The first South Korean flag was created in 1882, before it was redesigned in 1948 and 1984. But all of its many incarnations have featured the *taegeuk* at its centre. The red top-half of the circle (yang) marks the positive forces in life, while the blue bottom-half (yin) marks the negative forces. The flag also features four black trigrams at its corners, which are from the *I Ching (Book of Changes)*, one of the oldest books from the Confucian Chinese classics. The *geon* (☰) represents the sky, *ri* (☲) symbolises fire, *gam* (☵) equals water, while *gon* (☷) is the earth. The white backdrop of the flag marks peace and purity. The movement of these four elements creates harmony around the *taegeuk*. The flag as a whole represents the vision of the country and its ongoing pursuit of peace, unity, balance and harmony in the world.

10 Fascinating Koreans

While some of these names might not be familiar to many outside of the Korean peninsula, below is a selection of ten of the most history-making iconic Korean figures that any native would know.

1. The Kings of K-pop

Most music fans will have heard of BTS – South Korea's answer to Britain's One Direction. Short for *Bangtan Sonyeondan* (which translates to Bulletproof Boy Scouts) this young seven-member K-pop sensation has been making history since its debut on the international music scene in 2017, after making their debut in 2013 in South Korea. Topping the biggest music charts of the US, including the *Billboard 200* for which they were the first Korean artists to do so, BTS is the first music act since The Beatles to have had three number one albums in less than a year. Their growing accolades include having the best-selling album in Korean history and the best-selling album of 2018 worldwide with their record *Map of the Soul: Persona*. They were recently featured among *Time* magazine's list of 100 Most Influential People in the World in 2019.

ABOVE: BTS arrive for the 4th Gaon Chart K-Pop Awards in 2015 at the Olympic Park in Seoul.

2. The Golfing Queen

Park Se Ri, the recently retired female golf legend, has been a trailblazer for the sport, sparking an army of female golfers to join the international LPGA Tours following the success of her career. Inducted into the World Golf Hall of Fame in 2007, Park is the youngest ever winner of the US Women's Open, a title achieved in 1998 at just 20 years of age.

3. The Dear Leader

Kim Jong Un, the North Korean leader referred to as 'Dear Leader' by the people of the North, probably needs no introduction. But many are also equally unfamiliar with some of the more surprisingly liberal elements of his background, including the early years of his education in the 1990s, believed to have been in Switzerland. He was described to have been a shy child who nursed an obsession with basketball and the American NBA (National Basketball Association), as well as computer games and Jackie Chan films.

ABOVE: Park Se Ri at Atunyote Golf Club in New York in 2012.

ABOVE: Actress Choi Eun Hee and her husband, the film director Shin Sang Ok.

4. The Lovers and the Despot

The late South Korean actress Choi Eun Hee and her late husband, the film director Shin Sang Ok, are among two of the most famous people abducted in North Korea in the late 1970s under the orders of Kim Jong Il, the former leader of the North who was keen to develop the country's film industry. Nearly a decade on, after carefully gaining Kim's trust, the couple managed a dramatic escape at the US embassy in Vienna on a work trip there in 1986. The incredible story of the couple's life inside North Korea has been the subject of several books and documentaries including 2016's *The Lovers & the Despot*, which aired on Netflix.

5. The Hollywood Shaker

Canadian actress Sandra Oh is one of the biggest South Korean success stories in Hollywood. But her backstory is what makes her worth a mention as it depicts a classic Korean family upbringing to which many Korean immigrants can relate. While raised by traditional immigrant parents who wanted her to pursue an academic career, such as a doctor or lawyer, Oh followed a different path by acting from the age of 15.

Despite parental opposition, she studied drama at the National Theatre School in Montreal and has added several history-making accolades to her name including the prestigious Cannes FIPA d'Or for Best Actress award as early as 1994. The spotlight got her roles in Hollywood films including the Oscar-winning *Sideways,* which led to her role as Dr Cristina Yang on the television series *Grey's Anatomy* in 2005, earning Oh her first Golden Globe win and various Screen Actors Guild and Emmy Award nominations.

In 2018, Oh made history by becoming the first Asian actress to be nominated for an Emmy in the Lead Actress in a Drama Series category for her role in the crime series *Killing Eve.* She also won the 2018 Golden Globe for Best Actress in a TV Drama, making history as the first woman of Asian descent to receive the nod. In the same year, she became the first-ever Asian woman to host the Golden Globes and made history yet again on the same night, becoming the first woman of Asian descent to win multiple Golden Globes.

6. The Peacemaker

Ban Ki Moon held one of the most influential global positions ever by a Korean in the modern age during his stint as the eighth United Nations Secretary-General from January 2007 to December 2016.

Born in South Korea in 1944 and educated at the country's top-ranking Seoul National University followed by a Master's degree at Harvard University in the US, the former Secretary-General was inspired by his native nation's rise from the ashes of war and poverty to fight world poverty. 'I grew up in war,' he once said, 'and saw the United Nations help my country to recover and rebuild. That experience was a big part of what led me to pursue a career in public service.'

He also brought climate change to the forefront of the global agenda (with one of his first major initiatives being the 2007 Climate Change Summit) and was a strong proponent of women's rights and gender equality. He launched the UN Women branch and increased the number of women in senior management positions within the UN by more than 40 percent, reaching the highest level in the history of the organisation.

7. Three Lungs Park

Park Ji Sung, the former professional football player who rose to fame during his time at Manchester United, helped put Korea on the map of the football world. Park is the most successful Asian player of the sport in history, as the first Asian footballer to have won the UEFA Champions League and play in a UEFA Champions League final, as well as the first Asian to have won the FIFA Club World Cup. His incredible stamina and endurance level during games was said to have earned him the nickname 'Three Lungs' Park. The South Korean player bagged 19 trophies throughout his illustrious career spanning football clubs in several nations outside South Korea before he was scouted by British football legend Sir Alex Ferguson in 2005 to play for Manchester United. His stint saw him win the Premier League four times as well as the 2007–2008 UEFA Champions League and the 2008 FIFA Club World Cup.

8. The Nelson Mandela of Korea

The late former president of South Korea Kim Dae Jung was considered the 'Nelson Mandela of South Korea', having been a political prisoner prior to his presidency from 1998 to 2003, before becoming the first Korean to receive a Nobel Peace Prize. Kim was awarded the prestigious prize for his work on democracy and human rights in South Korea, particularly for his work on relations with North Korea during his time in office, which saw a historic summit take place with North Korea's former leader Kim Jong II in 2000. Kim was described as South Korea's 'first left-wing president' by the US Embassy in Seoul on the day of his death in 2009, highlighting his legacy of political reform and liberal policies.

9. The Revolutionary

The aforementioned Ahn Chang Ho (also known as Dosan) was a pioneer on both sides of the pond. Ahn moved to San Francisco with his wife in 1902 and they were the first Korean married couple to emigrate to the US at the time. Ahn was a strong defender of human rights and social reform both on American and Korean soil. He became the first-ever Asian from the Far East to be inducted into the International Civil Rights Walk of Fame, recognised for his civil rights work in Korea in the fight against Japan during the early 20th century as well as for his work on immigration and labor issues for Koreans in the US. Ahn's two children, raised in the US, also went on to become pioneers in their own right. Dosan's son Philip Ahn became the first Korean American film actor to be honoured with a star on the Hollywood Walk of Fame, while his sister Susan Ahn Cuddy was the first Asian–American woman to join the US Navy in 1942.

ABOVE: Park Ji Sung celebrates a goal for Manchester United in 2011.

ABOVE: Dosan Ahn Chang Ho in the 1920s.

10. The Devoted Daughter

The female protagonist of a famous story from Korean folklore forms the embodiment of filial piety, which is so central to Korean culture. Shimchung is the daughter of an old blind farmer who was told by a monk that he would receive his sight if he delivered 300 sacks of rice to his temple. At the end of the day, the farmer was distraught realising he didn't have enough rice. So Shimchung makes a deal with merchants at the harbour who were in need of a young girl to sacrifice to the God of the Sea, who they feared had been angered. Shimchung agrees to offer herself as a sacrifice in exchange for the remaining rice her father needs to gain his sight. Sadly, her father didn't gain his sight even after he delivered the rice to the temple, and was left heartbroken to have lost his daughter. Meanwhile deep in the ocean waters, Shimchung meets the God of the Sea, who is moved by her pious act and sends her back to land alive inside a giant orchid. She eventually meets the king of the land who falls in love with her and hosts a party for blind men in the local village, where she has a fateful reunion with her father, during which he miraculously receives his sight. This fictional character has become synonymous with deep devotion of any form, especially the familial kind, in Korean culture.

THE KOREAN SPIRIT

Relationships
and Social Life

Family dynamics

Let's face it. Families are complicated, regardless of your background, and it's no different for Korean families. The dynamics of any relationship, be it between family, friends or lovers, is so specific to people and their shared circumstances. But there are some common understandings passed down through generations of tradition that can be traced in many Korean families. How strongly they resonate in any given Korean household differs from family to family.

As mentioned earlier, one undisputed element is that of filial piety (having the utmost respect for your parents and other elders in your life), which is at the core of Confucian teachings that are deeply rooted in Korean culture. This ultimate respect naturally dictates the dynamics within Korean families and is played out in everyday life.

Obviously in modern-day South Korea, family structures and relationships have evolved with the times, but some old-school aspects of Korean family life and upbringing do linger and still form at least part of the (if not the entire) bedrock of family interactions.

Jeong (정)

Relationships and social interactions among Koreans, be it platonic, romantic or among family, are rooted in *jeong* (정), which is a word that I feel is unique to the Korean language. The closest English translation would be a close bond or deep connection and feelings of closeness, familiarity or attachment. There's a saying in Korean that goes 'Jeong is scarier than love' (사랑보다 정이 더 무 섭다), meaning it's harder to cut off *jeong* than it is to cut off the feelings between two lovers who have broken up, which highlights the depth of *jeong* that runs deep in any relationship.

Koreans are known to have a lot of *jeong* and in this chapter I'll unpack some of the relationships and interactions among them, as well as the various fundamental aspects of social life and events celebrated among Koreans.

RIGHT: **Family visiting Bulguksa Temple in Gyeongju.**

Parents

In a traditional Korean family setting, the relationship between parents and their children and how kids are raised are quite fundamentally different from that which you might see within a typical Western family model.

In many Western homes, as children get older they are taught to be independent from their parents, so that they can be financially self-sufficient but also in order to develop their sense of self and individuality. When children become adults, most parents are expected to respect the decisions they make, regardless of whether they agree or disagree with their children's life choices. These clear boundaries between a parent and a child and the healthy distance in the parent-child relationship are seen as a social norm and even beneficial. But in Korean families, these boundaries can be less clear and the parent–child relationship is more enmeshed. Even after children have grown up, their parents would expect them to be obedient to them. Any form of disobedience as an adult would be seen just as disrespectful as from young children.

For example, when it comes to marriage (which I speak about in more detail later in this chapter), it would be considered defiant to marry someone who isn't approved by your parents. That's not to say that Koreans only marry people that are approved by their parents, but to go against your parents' wishes in any way is seen as being defiant, more so than it would be in Western society. The notion of independence in some traditional Korean families can be seen as being inconsiderate of the family and sometimes even a rejection and abandonment of the family.

To give another example, children in most Western societies often aspire to move out of the family home as soon as they are financially able, but in traditional Korean families, there is an unspoken expectation for children to look after their parents as they get older. Therefore, it wouldn't be uncommon to see many still living with their parents as working adults or even after they get married – this can be the case mostly with sons, as daughters are considered to leave the family when they get married and join their husband's family unit.

There's a saying in Korean that roughly translates to 'sticking together means staying alive, while separating means death', which exemplifies just how vital family togetherness is perceived to be in traditional Korean family settings. In some Korean families, once you begin working, it's even considered customary to give your first-ever salary payment to your mother, as a symbol of gratitude towards her for giving birth to you and raising you. Those who live with their parents might even hand over their monthly salary to their mothers, because in some families it isn't unusual for mothers to manage all family finances, though this practice is rarer in the modern age.

But it's another example of how the family is seen as an entire unit. So the payment that a child brings home is seen rightfully as something that should go towards the entire family. Even when children get older and have formed their own families, it's not unusual to see children give their parents monthly *yong-dohn* (용돈), which means pocket money or allowance.

Siblings

Sibling relationships tend to be less enmeshed than that between parents and children, but older siblings are to be respected and obeyed by younger siblings. It would be rude to talk back to an older sibling (though that doesn't mean this sort of behaviour doesn't happen at all). On the other hand, older siblings are expected to look after and care for their younger siblings, and it wouldn't be unusual for older siblings to have a say in the lives of their younger siblings, in the same way a parent does.

ABOVE: Families taking a stroll in a park in Seoul.

Traditionally speaking, the eldest son – called the *jangnam* (장남) or if the oldest child is a daughter, the *jangnyeo* (장녀) – bears the greatest responsibility. There is an unspoken expectation for the eldest son to become the head of the household when he grows up. He is expected to look after his parents when they get older, even if the younger siblings may have fled the nest. *Jangnams* are often expected to choose a stable career path and feel a greater pressure to be successful in life because of the responsibility they are given.

Both *jangnams* and *jangnyeos* have a greater burden to look after their parents than their younger siblings. But traditionally, all daughters are considered outsiders as soon as they get married, since they are joining their husband's family and are obligated to their in-laws more than their own families.

Because of such obligations, it isn't uncommon to hear of parents favouring their eldest son, or sons in general, over daughters, as sons will carry the family bloodline forward. Male-to-female ratio at birth is still tilted toward males in Korea, with many families having multiple children in order to ensure they have more sons than daughters. Some will continue producing children until they have a son if they are a house full of daughters.

Wider family

It's not unusual for extended Korean families to live together, though this model has been in decline due to a number of socio-economic reasons. Back in the day, the head of large extended families under one roof would be the father or the grandfather of the household. But in the modern age, the nuclear family is more the norm.

As always, any elders in your extended family are to be respected in the same way that you respect your parents, even if you don't have a very close relationship with any of your uncles, aunts or grandparents. However, you wouldn't be expected to look after aunts and uncles or cousins in the same close way that you would your parents, siblings or grandparent.

But there are social family etiquettes that would be expected of you (though not always fulfilled, since there are always exceptions). For example, it can be considered rude not to visit your extended family during certain major holidays or to arrive empty handed, so most would bring a box of fruit or some other food when visiting.

What's in a name?

Age difference is a big deal among Koreans, even if that difference is only of a year or less, and showing respect starts with the way you address people who are older than you. There are specific ways that different people are to be addressed. For example, you would never call out the name of your older brother or sister when referring to them directly or in the third person. Instead, there are titles that translate to 'older brother' or 'older sister'. These are also used to refer to any person who is a few years older than you (but not someone old enough to be your parent, aunt, uncle or grandparent) regardless of whether they are blood-relations. Some of these titles are also used by couples as endearing terms towards each other.

It is worth noting that these titles are used for people with whom you are familiar. When you're speaking to anyone else you don't know very well, you would use formal tone words (존댓말, pronounced *jone det mal*). Names in Korean can be addressed in a formal tone by adding the letters 씨 (pronounced *shee*) at the end. For example, if a stranger were to say my name, they would say '*Soo Kim*씨', which is the equivalent of saying 'Miss Soo Kim'. Many other words or phrases in Korean can be made formal by adding either 요 (pronounced *yoh*) or a few other letter combinations (which vary according to the word) at the end of it. For example, an informal way of saying hello is 안녕 (pronounced *ahn nyung*), while the formal tone of hello is 안녕하세요 (pronounced *ahn nyung ha sae yoh*).

These titles can be used either alone or be placed just after the person's name when you are calling out to them. Below are the different basic titles you would use in conversations and interaction:

누나 (pronounced *noo nah*) *or* 누님 (*noo neem*) – this title is only used by a man who is referring to or speaking to a woman who is a few years older than himself. So if a man who is younger than myself was calling me or referring to me, he would say *noo-nah* or *Soo noo-nah*.

언니 (pronounced *uhn nee*) – this title is only used by a woman who is referring to or speaking to a woman who is a few years older than herself.

형 (pronounced *hyeung*) or 형님 (*hyeung neem*) – this title is only used by a man who is referring to or speaking to a man who is a few years older than himself. *Hyeung* is used when you're referring to someone not that much older than you, while *hyeung neem* is used when you're referring to someone fairly significantly older than you (but not old enough to be your dad or uncle or grandfather).

오빠 (pronounced *oppah*) – this title is only used by a woman who is referring to or speaking to a man who is a few years older than herself.

How to date a Korean

It's a set up (but not always)

Relying on friends and family for referrals on potential partners is common practice in Korean culture. Approaching someone directly, especially a complete stranger, and asking the person to go on a date is rare, but that's not to say it doesn't happen at all.

Generally, dating begins at a later age than in the West, where people as young as high-school age will embark on somewhat serious, exclusive relationships. But high school in Korea, as mentioned in the previous chapter, entails a lot of high stress due to studies in preparation for university, so there really isn't any time for dating, let alone personal time. Korean parents don't usually allow their children to date until they begin university.

Sogaeting (소개팅), a term Koreans made up by combining the word 'meeting' and 'sogae' which means 'introduction' or 'to introduce', is a blind date set up by mutual friends, colleagues or other connections and it's a common way many of the younger generation tend to meet potential love interests in Korea.

University students often like to do 'meetings' (미팅) instead, which is a group blind date between a handful of guys and girls who hangout. You might see this taking place in a cafe, where you'll see girls sitting on one side of the table and the same number of boys sitting opposite on the other. They tend to eventually pair off as the group date progresses.

There are, of course, people who meet their romantic partners by chance but blind dates are very common. In many ways, blind dates cater to the conservative nature of many traditional Koreans who can be both shy and not forthcoming when it comes to dating. For the more inexperienced Koreans, it eliminates either party from having to make the nerve-wracking awkward first move to express their romantic interest in the other. With a blind date, the meeting is already arranged and both parties know they are there in the interest of pursuing a romantic connection, so there's no guesswork involved.

More formal arrangements known as *maht-sun* (맞선), which are set ups by a matchmaker, still exist. In many Korean television dramas, you see scenes of parents in wealthy families using a matchmaker to find a suitor for their son or daughter. Some young adults are open to these arranged meetings, which can eventually lead to marriage after a short period of getting to know each other. Some *maht-suns* and even marriages are forced in the sense that the parents may have wanted it to happen more than the two suitors themselves. *Maht-suns* tend to happen among the older crowd. Many parents with older children who are single tend to try to get them to go on a *maht-sun* and it's common to find couples from the older generations who have met through a *maht-sun*.

Dating taboos and customs

Koreans can be quite old-fashioned, so when it comes to who pays for the meal or other activities on a date, it is expected that the man would foot the bill, at least for the first few dates. But once you get to know each other over a period of time, many couples tend to take turns paying or some other system between the two tends to fall naturally into place.

It's still considered taboo to live together and sleep together before marriage among most traditional Koreans of the older generation. While living together before marriage isn't completely unheard of in Korean society – and certainly happens more these days – there is still a sense of taboo or even shame around

LEFT: **Young couples take selfies at the Cherry Blossom festival in Yeouido district, Seoul.**

it among traditional Koreans. Most Korean parents would gasp and raise their eyebrows, at the very least, at seeing it happen among their children or others. The same reaction would apply to having children before marriage.

The older generation of Koreans tend to believe only two people who are committed to each other through marriage should be living together. The Western concept of 'try before you buy' behind cohabitation which views living together as a testing stage before marriage doesn't really exist in Korean culture. Culturally there is still a sense of shyness and conservativeness about sexual relations in general, and certainly before marriage. You won't see many steamy kissing sessions in public or couples being overly tactile in a sensual way in the presence of others (especially your elders, as it would be considered extremely rude and almost vulgar to do so). Holding hands and a quick peck on the cheek or lips are more commonplace when it comes to most public displays of affection.

Meeting a partner's parents tends to only happen when you're at a serious stage in the relationship, with marriage on the cards. That typical scenario in many Western films where a guy might casually pop in to say hello to the parents while you're there to either drop the girl off or pick her up doesn't happen very much. You're more likely to visit each other's parents to introduce yourself formally as an official girlfriend or boyfriend and meet the family.

The perfect match

While Korean couples might not be passionately kissing each other while out and about, they are very affectionate and like to publicly express it in other ways. It's not unusual to see couples wearing matching t-shirts (커플티 – a 'couple tee') or any other matching garment, from jumpers to jackets or even something small such as matching key rings. Matching shirts are commonly seen on Koreans on honeymoon, especially at Jeju Island, the classic honeymoon destination for Korean locals.

Matching clothes is one way to signify that you are a couple but it is mostly about just being cute together. Korean dating culture tends to be expressive in a very cute (some might say super cheesy) manner, so matching garments are right in line with that type of cute culture.

RIGHT: A couple wearing head to toe matching outfits on the street near Gyeongbokgung Palace. NEXT PAGE: Love padlocks left by couples at Namsan Tower.

As Koreans tend to be quite conservative when it comes to coupledom, wearing matching outfits is for them a more endearing, less provocative way of indicating couple status and showing their affection for each other.

Anniversaries

The 100-day and 1,000-day anniversaries are big ones for Korean couples. The 100th day mark is significant as it usually means you're getting more serious or are an official couple. Many go to great lengths to make grand gestures on such days, both in public and in private. One example is the many love padlocks left at Namsan Tower in Seoul – similar to the ones placed at several bridges in Paris and other famous spots around the world.

For the 100th-day anniversaries, it wouldn't be uncommon to have 100 roses delivered to you or for rose petals to be scattered across a large, open field spelling out your name or some other romantic message, or for candles to be lit along the ground to form the shape of a giant heart. To the outside world, it can all seem very cringeworthy, but that's Korean dating for you in a nutshell! There probably isn't any act that would be considered too much or too cheesy when it comes to celebrating the anniversary of a relationship in Korea, so hopeless romantics can rest assured nothing is off the table when it comes to grand gestures.

Generally Koreans tend to be thoughtful and quite romantic when they are dating someone or in a relationship (or they endeavour to be). How expressive they are of these qualities varies according to the individual and the relationship.

Valentine's Day and White Day

Valentine's Day is celebrated on 14 February, as it is in Western societies, but in South Korea it's a day when women are expected to make the romantic gesture (whether that be in the form of chocolates, flowers or other gifts). But on White Day, which is celebrated on 14 March, just a month after Valentine's Day, the roles are reversed and the onus is on the man in the relationship to give gifts to the woman. White Day was said to have first been created and celebrated in Japan before it spread to other countries in Asia, where it is celebrated in the same fashion as in Korea.

On White Day, men tend to present white-themed items to their partners, such as white chocolate or sometimes even white lingerie (which I'd say is probably among the few openly racy or risque expressions you might see among Korean couples).

Korean marriage

Throughout Korea's history, marriage has been considered one of, if not, the most important and sacred rites of passage a person goes through in life. Once marriage has been agreed, the meeting of the parents of both parties is also important. The reason for the significance of this meeting is because Koreans see marriage as not just two people becoming one unit, but as two households coming together, which ties into why parents' approval is considered important.

Many traditional Koreans, especially from the older generation, such as my own mother, say you need to marry someone that matches your *joo jeh* (주제 – circumstances) and *soo joon* (수준 – level), believing that marriage works best when two people come from similar backgrounds financially, sociologically and so forth. Bearing that in mind, many older Koreans have tended to prefer their children date and marry other Koreans. But interracial dating and marriages have become more frequent today, with the growing influence of Western culture in Korean society in the 21st century and many Korean parents aren't as opposing of it as previous generations may have been.

It's more common for the man to propose to the woman than vice versa. Afterwards, the couple usually meets with each other's parents to announce their intention to marry and seek their permission and blessings. But as mentioned earlier, there are couples who marry each other even in the face of opposition from their parents.

Engagement periods tend to be relatively short in Korean society or not as long as you might see in many Western societies, where they can last for a year or more. Engagement parties aren't that common, especially since engagement periods are not long, and couples opt to save their money to put it towards the wedding instead. But wealthier families might still hold an engagement ceremony. Weddings in Korea can be planned very quickly, with many wedding halls offering a package deal taking care of every element of the day, from the flowers to the photographs and beyond. So a long engagement period for the sake of organising the wedding is not seen as necessary.

Rings are exchanged between the couple during the wedding ceremony but giving the woman an engagement ring at the time of proposal isn't traditionally part of Korean custom. However, with the growing influence of Western culture on Korean society, some couples in modern times do practise the engagement ring ritual. Many couples also wear 'couple rings' even before they are married (some even as soon as the 100th day mark or another anniversary) to signify they are together, meaning an engagement ring can seem redundant.

The ceremony

Historically Korean wedding ceremonies were elaborate and involved extravagant traditional wedding garments worn by the bride and groom. It was usually held in the small front courtyard of the bride's family home, so many people from the neighbourhood would try to take a peek over the walls to catch a glimpse of the ceremony and the bride in her best clothes and makeup, which included two distinct red circular patches on both cheeks and a sparkling headpiece.

A large mat would be laid across the yard and a table placed on it, filled with various food, drink and centrepiece items, such as a pair of wooden Mandarin duck carvings to symbolize bountiful children, peace and fidelity. The groom would travel on horseback to the bride's house on the day of the wedding. The ceremony would entail a series of formal bows between the groom and bride, who was assisted by a female helper on either side to bow down to the floor in her elaborate wedding gown. The wedding night was spent at the bride's family home and the next morning the groom would take his wife back to his house where they would begin their married life. She would travel there in a *gama* (가마 – a sedan chair), which was manually carried by a group of porters.

Modern-day weddings in Korea follow the Western tradition, with the bride and groom in a white wedding dress and tuxedo, and the bride being walked down the aisle by her father. But many weddings still incorporate some traditional aspects, such as the *paebaek* (폐백), which is a wedding blessing ceremony. Traditionally it was a pre-wedding ritual where the bride is introduced to the groom's family in a formal setting but these days it often takes place on the wedding day, just after the reception.

The *paebaek* ritual sees the bride and groom wearing traditional Korean garments known as *hanbok* (한복), some even choose to wear the actual elaborate Korean wedding gowns worn back in the day. The bride and groom simultaneously bow facedown to several elderly members of the extended family, who each take turns sitting on floor mats just beyond a table set up with food. The bowing involves placing the front sides of both hands on top of each other against your forehead and bowing down to the ground until your hands

RIGHT: A couple poses for wedding photos in a park in Seoul.

touch the floor, after which you sit in an upright position but with hands to your sides and head tilting slightly downwards out of respect for your elders. Modern-day *paebaeks* involve bowing to elders on both sides of the family, rather than just the groom's family as was the practice in the past.

The elders share words of wisdom and blessings for the marriage once the couple sits down in front of them after their bow. The elders then throw a handful of chestnuts and dates (which represent children) from the table, which are caught by the couple by extending the bride's long cloak between them, to wish them plenty of offspring in the future.

Another aspect of the *paebaek*, usually after all the bowing to the elders is done, sees the bride and groom hold up a date together, with each of their mouths holding one end of the date using their teeth. They then simultaneously take a bite into the date and whoever ends up with the seed of the date in their mouth is said to be the one who will hold the power in the marriage.

A rather unusual ritual that some modern weddings may include is the beating of the groom's feet. The groomsmen, or other family members usually from the bride's side, hold the groom's feet together while he lays flat on the floor and they each take turns hitting the bottom of his feet using a small stick

ABOVE: Chestnuts thrown as a blessing during the *paebaek* ritual.

or a large, whole dried fish that's as hard as a stick. It's meant to be a test of the groom's strength and character to endure the beating and to increase his vitality for the wedding night. It can even be seen as a bit of a hazing ritual before the groom officially takes his bride away in marriage. Sounds devious, I know, but more than anything it's just meant to be a bit of fun and ends up being a comical portion towards the end of the wedding rituals.

Married life

Back in the day, it was expected for the wife to leave her own family to join her husband's family and devote her life to his family and its elders. They would become her family and her elders through marriage and therefore also her responsibility. Of course, this isn't always the case in modern times and many couples live on their own these days, but there are some brides who do follow tradition and end up living with their parents-in-law after marriage.

The traditional division of roles between man and woman can be seen in some of the terms that have been used to refer to either person. One of the Korean terms referring to a husband is *bahk-ghat-yangban* (바깥양반), which translates to 'nobleman of the outside', meaning the husband handles external

ABOVE: Wooden ducks used in traditional Korean weddings.

affairs and matters outside the household, such as bringing income to sustain the family. Among the terms for a wife in Korean is *jeep sah rahm* (집사람 – person of the house) or *ah-neh* (아내). The '*neh*' here is spelled the same as in the Korean word *neh boo* (내부), which means 'inside' or 'internal', inferring that the wife's role is to be in charge of internal affairs and matters regarding the home, such as cooking and other housework. It wouldn't be unusual for the wife to collect the monthly pay cheques from her husband's work and manage the household funds and budget.

As with various other aspects of Korean culture, the modern age has seen married life structures evolve, so there are many households where both the husband and wife earn an income out of necessity or want and both often pursue active careers.

Conscription in South Korea

From around 1957, every man in South Korea has been required to serve in the military, as outlined by the Constitution of South Korea and the Military Service Act. Women can volunteer for military service but are not required to serve. The length of time served varies according to the branch of the military (army, marines, navy or air force) but it tends to be around two years.

By the age of 18, every man is enlisted for 'first citizen service', which means he is liable to fulfill his military duty but not yet required to serve. When a man turns either 19 or 20, he undergoes a draft physical examination to determine whether he is capable of military service. Men must fulfill their military duties by no later than around 28 years of age.

There are several levels of military service, so not every man may be placed on active duty service, depending on the needs of the military each year. At what level you serve is determined by the results of your physical examination, which can include exemption from service if you are suffering from an illness or deemed not physically well enough to serve.

Some men may be placed in the health department, if they are doctors or have some other medical background, or be put within some other area of expertise. Those determined not eligible for active duty service following the physical examination may serve in an administrative department or in other support roles.

Life's milestones and celebrations

In Korean culture, the clock starts the day you are conceived rather than the day you leave the womb. So when people say their age, you could subtract one year to understand what that would be in most Western societies. In addition, it's customary in Korea to add another year to age when the calendar hits 1 January. So, while birthdays are celebrated on the actual dates that people are born, one's age doesn't change until 1 January. People use their Korean age in everyday life, while all legal paperwork lists their international age. Confusing? Well, to simplify things, most Koreans tend to ask each other what year they were born to ascertain how old someone is in day-to-day life.

Here are some of the important milestones celebrated in Korean society.

Sae-i-rae (세이레) **marks the celebration of the first 21 days since the birth of a child.** Historically, a mother and newborn did not leave their rooms and stayed indoors in order to prevent catching any disease and preserve their health while in recovery from the birth. Visitors were not allowed in order to protect their health. The mother would eat *miyeokguk* (미역국) a seaweed soup with rice for the nutritional benefits of seaweed, which include iodine for thyroid function, iron, copper and zinc among other vitamins and minerals, as well as antioxidants. This soup is considered the 'birthday soup' and is eaten on one's birthday or by a new mother just after giving birth even in modern-day Korea. The mother also eats *baekseolgi* (백설기), which is a white rice cake symbolic of sacredness. Today infant death rates are much lower with the advancement of medical science and technology. Therefore, the mother and newborn are allowed to leave the hospital or their home and have visitors just days after the birth. Since a baby is very likely to survive the first 21 days nowadays, *sae-i-rae* isn't observed as much, if at all, among Koreans in the modern age.

Baek-il (백일), **which means 100 days, marks a celebration of a baby's first 100 days of life.** Traditionally, the celebration involved offering prayer and thanksgiving for protecting the child until the 100th day to the *samshin*, which translates to 'three gods' in Korean and refers to the three goddesses of childbirth in Korean Shamanism. They are sometimes called *samshin halmoni*, meaning 'three grandmother goddesses'. *Baek-il* entails eating rice cakes (떡, *dduck*) and other Korean delicacies to pray for the child's good fortune, wealth and longevity. It's believed that if the rice cakes are shared with 100 others it will guarantee the longevity of the child, so many families share rice cakes with several neighbours and family members to reach that 100 mark in honour of the 100 days. In modern times, the *baek-il* celebration tends to just be a gathering of friends and family for a party to celebrate the birthday, so the ritualistic prayers aren't practised as much.

Dol (돌) marks the first year since the baby's birth and is the biggest of the milestones celebrated for babies. A big *dol janchi* (돌잔치) – *janchi* meaning 'feast' – is held, with lots of family and friends invited. Historically, the likelihood of a child surviving harsh weather conditions and seasonal changes, among other variables, was deemed to be low, having survived a full year was a big feat to be celebrated and grateful for. But this tradition continues today, despite the low infant mortality rate with the advancement of medical facilities.

For the *dol janchi*, the child is dressed up in a traditional *dol bok* (돌복) outfit, which includes a jacket, a hat with a long train, specific socks and trousers (skirts for girls). The jacket features a long belt that wraps around the baby twice to symbolize longevity. The outfit also comes with a *doljoomuhni* (돌주머니 – a small pouch) made of silk, which symbolizes good fortune.

Historically, the first part of the celebration involved praying over a table of food as an offering to the *sanshin* (산신 – mountain god) and the *samshin* (삼신 – three gods) to ask for their continued protection for the baby's health, longevity and good luck in life. The table showcases several different types of rice cakes, including the *baeksolgi dduck*, just like during the 100 day celebration. Other rice cakes might include the *moojeegae dduck*, which is a rainbow-coloured rice cake. The table also displays various objects, which can include a pencil and/or a paintbrush for writing Korean calligraphy, a book, an envelope of money, a long thread of string, a needle, a ruler and scissors.

The prayer portion is not practised much these days but one traditional aspect that does remain is the *doljabee* (돌잡이), which is the main part of the event. It sees the child's future being determined by what he or she grabs from the table of objects. The child is placed on a mat in front of the table and whichever object he or she grabs first symbolizes the child's future. The pencil, book or paintbrush mean the child will be very intelligent, while grabbing the

ABOVE: Traditional *Dol* Table for a first birthday party.
BELOW: Traditional *hanboks* worn for a *Dol* party.

money or rice cakes means they will be very wealthy and won't ever go hungry. The needle, ruler and scissors mean they will be dexterous and skillful, while the thread of string means the child will live a long life.

These days some of these objects might be replaced by others that better symbolize the things the parents would want for their child. For example, some might place a stethoscope on the table in the hope that their child will become a doctor.

Hwangap (환갑) **celebrates a person's 60th birthday.** Historically, the number 60 represented a complete cycle of life according to the Chinese cosmic calendar, therefore 60 holds significance in Korean culture (much like people celebrating the 50th year mark as a big birthday). Usually there is a *hwangap janchi* held to celebrate with family and friends over food and drink.

Chilsoon (칠순) **celebrates the 70th birthday** and, again, living beyond 60 (which, as mentioned above, is considered the completion of your life cycle) is seen as a joyous miracle to celebrate. Similar to the 60th birthday, there is an extravagant *chilsoon janchi* held with lots of family and friends invited.

Other celebrations

Shinjung (신정 – **New Year's Day**) – the first of January is a national holiday in the sense that the country gets a day off work but it isn't celebrated in the way that the Lunar New Year is celebrated.

Seolnal (설날 – **Lunar New Year**) – this major event coincides with Chinese New Year, celebrating the start of a new year according to the Chinese lunar calendar, so it takes place in late January or early February. It is among the biggest dates on the Korean cultural calendar. During this period, people celebrate by wearing the traditional Korean *hanbok* (한복) garments and visit several relatives' homes bringing them gifts and bowing down to their elders (as a bride and groom does for their *paebaek* ritual), listening to their words of wisdom for the new year ahead. Young children in each family also participate in the bowing, after which the elders give them each some money. A traditional savoury rice-cake soup topped with dried seaweed strips called *dduck guk* (떡국) is eaten on this day.

LEFT: South Koreans wearing traditional clothes celebrate Lunar New Year at Gyeongbokgung Royal Palace in Seoul.

Uh rhee nee nal (어린이날 – Children's Day) takes place on 5 May and it's meant to be a day of treats for all kids. Children are given gifts by adults or go on excursions to various fun venues such as theme parks.

Uh buh ee nal (어버이날 – Parents' Day) is marked on 8 May and is a day of appreciation for all parents. There is no separate mother's day or father's day, so this day serves to celebrate both parents. Celebrations involve gift giving and meals out or at home.

Hyeongchoongil (현충일 – Memorial Day) is marked on 6 June. This is a day of remembrance for Korean veterans who died while serving in the military and the Korean independence movement during the country's period of Japanese occupation. This historical holiday sees the raising of the Korean flag along roads, and over homes and buildings across the country.

Gwangbokjeol (광복절) – on 15 August, celebrates liberation from Japanese rule in 1945. This is another historical holiday that sees the raising of the Korean flag across the country.

Chuseuk (추석 – commonly considered Korean Thanksgiving) is celebrated on the 15th day of the 8th month of the lunar calendar, so it usually takes place in

ABOVE: Visitors celebrating *Chuseuk* wearing traditional *Hanbok* pose for photos at Gyeongbokgung palace in Seoul.

September or October. It marks the celebration of a good harvest that year and is centred around feasting on traditional foods and making *songpyeon* (송편 – a half-moon-shaped, sweet rice cake). Traditionally, *songpyeon* is made together as a family the night before *chuseuk*, because there's a lot to make but it's also meant to be a time of family bonding and a fun aspect for children. There's a Korean superstition that says if you make pretty looking *songpyeon*, you'll give birth to beautiful children.

Sung tahn jeol (성탄절 – Christmas) is celebrated in Korea but it isn't the lavish affair that it is in the West and it doesn't hold the same significance in terms of holiday rankings (*chuseuk* and *seolnal* are the two biggest holidays in South Korea). It is a national holiday in that everyone gets time off from work and schools are closed sometime between Christmas Eve and a day or two after Christmas.

However, there are some fundamental differences when compared with how Christmas is celebrated in Western countries. Christmas decorations, for example, are seen in major shopping areas and in some churches but it's not common to decorate your home with sparkling Christmas tinsel and baubles galore. It's also not a family-oriented holiday but more of a couple-centric, romantic day. So rather than spending Christmas Eve and Christmas Day with family, most spend it with their other half or even friends. Gift exchange between friends and family is traditionally not big nor required, although with the growing influence of Western culture it has become more commonplace. But even then, people tend to stick to just one gift per person for a handful of people in their circle of loved ones. Many times they opt for giving money in an envelope. It wouldn't be unusual to forgo a gift exchange but it's usually done between couples more than anything.

Christmas is another reason to have a feast of course, but the typical foods you might find in a Western home are not on the menu during Christmas in Korea. There are no Christmas-specific foods eaten and most tend to go out to eat, rather than have a big homemade family meal at home. Restaurants tend to be quite packed during Christmas because many choose to eat out with friends or their significant other. Those who do eat at home with friends or family just have different Korean dishes.

Christmas is a more of a big deal and celebrated in the way you'd expect in Western countries in areas of Seoul such as Itaewon, where there is a higher population of Western communities. Probably the most Christmas-like activity in South Korea that takes place around Christmas are Christmas carols. You do see groups of carol singers making the rounds singing Christmas songs. And children do get excited over Santa Claus (known as Grandpa Santa among kids in Korea), anticipating receiving gifts from Santa on Christmas Day or visiting Santa at a department store, as you might see in the West.

Korean superstitions and symbols

Below are some unusual Korean superstitions that many still believe in.

- **Never write names in red**: red lettering was used to write the names of the deceased. Writing the name of a living person in red is a bad omen and is believed to wish death or even bring death upon that person.

- **Unlucky 4:** the number 4 – *sah* (사) is associated with death because it is spelled the same as the first half of the Korean word for death, which is *sah-mang* (사망). Therefore, the number 4 is considered an unlucky number, so much so that most, if not all, building lifts in Korea use the letter F instead of 4 to indicate the fourth floor.

- **Stick with taffy:** many students eat *yeot* (엿), a type of Korean sticky taffy made from glutinous rice, on the day of any exams to have their knowledge and luck stick with them. On the other hand, they are meant to avoid slippery foods like seaweed soup or noodles, as these are meant to make your luck slip away.

- **No shoes for lovers:** gifting shoes to your significant other means your lover will run away from you in Korean culture, so it's bad luck to do so. In other shoe references, there's a saying in Korean – *goh moo shin guh ggoo roh shint dah* (고무신 거꾸로 신다) – that translates to 'wearing your rubber shoes backwards' and it specifically refers to a woman running away with another man while her boyfriend is serving in the army (which all men in South Korea are required to do – see box, page 138). It originates from the days when most people wore rubber shoes and refers to mens' fear that their wives or girlfriends would leave them while they were fulfilling their military duties. This saying comes from describing a situation where a woman gets caught cheating on her husband or boyfriend when he returns from the military unexpectedly and she ends up putting her shoes on backwards as she scrambles away.

- **...or chicken wings:** there seems to be a lot of paranoia around infidelity in Korean culture. They say you shouldn't feed your boyfriend or husband any chicken wings, as they will fly away from you and have an affair with another woman.

- **No whistling at night:** they say this will summon ghosts and evil spirits.

- **Don't shake your leg:** they say this shakes the good luck and fortune out of you. It's also generally considered rude to shake your leg, especially in front of elders.

- **Dream about pigs:** symbolizing wealth and good fortune, it's considered good luck if you come across pigs in your dreams.

Hobbies

Koreans work hard (which I further explain later in this chapter) but they also love to play hard. When free time beckons, South Koreans have a number of recreational activities that they're very keen on, from sports and spending time in nature to shopping and everything in between. And whatever the activity, eating and/or drinking is a key part of the enjoyment of the experience.

Fishing: a survey in 2017 by the country's culture and tourism institute revealed fishing was South Korea's favourite hobby. Fishing is a typical hobby among men, especially dads in South Korea, who sometimes spend days away on fishing trips, either solo or with fellow fish-fanatic friends. Fishing, along with agriculture, was among the main industries of the country until industrialization and urbanization in the 1960s. But today it has evolved into a favourite pastime.

Hiking: it's no surprise that Koreans love hiking, with a country mostly covered by forest land and home to 22 national parks. The capital city itself is enclosed

ABOVE: A fisherman at a harbour in Seogwipo, Jeju Island. NEXT PAGE: A hiker at Bukhansan mountain, Seoul.

by the ridges of four mountains (Bugaksan, Naksan, Namsan and Inwangsan) along the UNESCO-designated Seoul City Wall.

But among the most popular spots for hiking is Bukhansan National Park. Located at the northern border of Seoul, it is the highest peak in the city's limits. With around five million visitors a year across an area spanning 30 square miles (80 sq km), the park was once listed in the Guinness Book of World Records as the world's 'Most Visited National Park Per Unit Area'. Seoraksan is another popular favourite outside the capital, located in the Gangwondo province, near the city of Sokcho. It is the third highest mountain in the country, forming part of the Taebaek mountain range.

Golfing: it's believed that golfing was first introduced to the country in the late 1890s by Englishmen working at one of the country's tourism organizations, who built a makeshift mini-golf course next to the Korean Customs Office. Through to the 1980s, the sport was seen as a game for wealthy people in the business world or government officials. But, in 1998, the emergence of the aforementioned Park Se Ri changed the face of golf in Korea forever. Park was a rookie player, who won the US Open that year, one of the five major golf championship titles she would win. Her career saw her enter the Golf Hall of Fame. Her success inspired several others, especially women, to take up the sport. In recent years, Korean women have dominated the sport, with around five of the top ten players of the LPGA tour being South Korean women. South Korea is among the top three markets for golf, after the US and Japan. It has around 450 golf courses, all of which are outside the capital and these courses are known for their lavish settings and extravagant facilities.

The sport is popular among both men and women at a recreational level, with there being lots of virtual golf courses available in the capital, as well as short-range walled golf practice centres. The launch of virtual golf courses from 2006, which are found on nearly every street in the capital, has seen an increase among young golfers in their 20s and 30s, while traditionally it's been more popular with the 40s age group and onwards, especially given it can be an expensive hobby.

PC bang (PC방): these online video gaming rooms are very popular in Korea, among youth, especially teenagers. These internet cafes allow them to participate in multiplayer online games with hundreds of thousands of other players around the world. The gaming industry is a billion dollar industry in

South Korea and PC bangs really took off after the launch of the computer game StarCraft back in 1998. In 2018, it was estimated that the gaming industry contributed around 11 trillion South Korean won to the country's economy. But the profits come at a cost to the health of teenagers and others who are addicted to online gaming, which has even resulted in the death of some gamers, who spent long hours in an internet cafe without eating much food.

Game addiction in South Korea has become so serious that the World Health Organization in 2019 voted to add 'gaming disorder' to its International Classification of Diseases. The classification will reportedly come into effect sometime in 2022 at the earliest and is causing much debate in the country due to the effect it will have on the profitable gaming industry.

Back in 2012, the country passed a law that banned those under 16 years of age from playing online games between 12 a.m. and 6 a.m., a law which cost the industry around 2.8 trillion won. Up to 16 percent of teenagers in the country are at risk of developing some form of game addiction, according to a survey of internet and smartphone use by the country's National Centre for Youth Internet Addiction Treatment (I think it says a lot that such an institution even exists). Some say it's a deeper issue than just an addiction to online gaming, with several of those addicted to gaming showing other mental health issues including depression.

But for now, PC bangs remain popular because for many students it's the only form of entertainment they can fit into their long hours of studying, with most students studying until around 9 p.m. or so, attending after-school prep academies. These internet cafes are also easily accessible due to their low cost, reportedly charging only around £2 or sometimes even less per hour in many places. So it's easy for students to spend long hours there.

Hwatoo (화투): this traditional Korean card game is also known as 'Go-Stop' (*Hwatoo* refers to the actual cards). It's said to be most comparable to casino in Western culture, so it is a fishing game where the object is to 'capture cards' by matching the cards from the hand you are given to the ones laid out in the open. It is played among two or three players at a time. There are 48 cards in the deck (four from each deck are pictured with a flower associated with a different month of the year, some of the cards have a picture of an animal or other design on them, which indicates a higher value).

The object is to capture as many matching cards as possible and you score points with each capture (and claim payment with chips equal to the score).

ABOVE: Traditional *Hwatoo* card deck featuring floral and animal designs.
BELOW: A *Baduk* board – a game that is around 3,000 years old.

Before the game begins, the players need to agree on a target score to which each player should aim and whoever reaches that score first wins the game. Throughout the game, you can choose to 'stop' playing if you think you've made sufficient captures and just collect payment then from the other players. But you risk having another player win the entire game by pulling out of the game. Or you can 'go' on and keep playing until the end of the game.

Baduk (바둑): this historic game is said to be the world's oldest board game, having been around for nearly 3,000 years. It's believed to have originated somewhere in China or the Himalayas, with some saying a game of *baduk* was once used to decide the fate of Tibet (China) when a Buddhist ruler challenged his opposer to a game to avoid battle and bloodshed. According to legend, the first emperor of China was said to have invented the game to help improve the mind of his not-so-fast-thinking son.

Regardless of exactly how it came to be, today the game is very popular in South Korea, China and Japan, where it was first introduced around 740 AD Japan was where the game really developed. To give you a picture of the level of strategy involved, it is described to be like four chess games happening at once on one board. It's similar to chess in that it involves a grid and two players taking turns placing stones (either black or white) on the board. But the stones are placed at the intersection of the lines, rather than inside the boxes. To put it very simply, the object of the game is to capture as many stones from your opponent by surrounding them with your own stones. The game and its rules are said to be much simpler than chess but it is just as, if not more, cerebral in terms of strategy.

The game is said to be played by around 50 million people in the Far East and in the past 15 years or so, South Korea has dominated international tournaments, according to the Korean Baduk Association. The game is very popular among the older generation.

Holidays

On average, South Koreans only get around 10–15 days of paid holiday per year. As a result, many opt to either go on trips domestically, such as to Jeju Island or elsewhere in Asia, such as Japan and parts of Southeast Asia including Vietnam and Thailand, to keep costs and journey times down. In recent years, Taipei in Taiwan, has become a popular holiday destination, along with China Hong Kong and Macau, joining other favourites such as the Thai capital Bangkok, as well as the Japanese cities of Osaka, Fukuoka and Tokyo.

The short amount of paid holiday in South Korea reflects the country's culture of long working hours. Employers are said to usually not approve of more than five or so consecutive days of holiday. The country was ranked to have the third highest average number of hours worked per worker in a year among the OECD countries, after Mexico and Costa Rica, in a 2018 report by the OECD. South Koreans were found to work nearly 500 hours more per year than workers in the UK and around 200 hours more than those in the US annually.

The previous maximum working week limit was set at 68 hours (not including weekends), but in 2018 the government passed a bill that came about as part of a campaign pushed by President Moon Jae In which brought the maximum down to 52 hours (which entails a maximum of 40 hours a week, plus a maximum of 12 hours of overtime allowed, including weekends).

Another holiday option that's been on the rise in recent years has been camping or glamping. Koreans love a bit of luxury, so it's no surprise that this trend has caught on in the country, where people can enjoy the benefits of being immersed in nature without compromising on comfort. There are a string of glamping sites and facilities dotted across the country's scenic parks.

In recent years, the capital has seen a rise in urban 'day camping' where city residents have been opting to camp out in the city's green spaces such as Yeouido Park, the largest park along the Han River in Seoul. They hang out there inside tents during the summer months as a budget, low-key camping option for those who don't have the time or money to get out of the city to larger glamping sites. But the city has issued curfews around these day-camping activities, in a bid to keep the parks clean, protect them from damage and also to discourage promiscuous behaviour in public. The tents are only allowed in certain areas of the park and need to be folded by 7 p.m. and must remain with their zips open at all times.

ABOVE: Glamping Architecture designed by ArchiWorkshop offers a
luxury camping experience in South Korea.

Friendships and going out

Friendships in Korea are important and the depth of that relationship is rooted in the Korean word for friend, which is *chingoo* (친구). The 'chin' in *chingoo* is the same 'chin' you see in the Korean word for being close with someone, which is *chinhae* (친해). So the bonds between friends in Korea are very close and run deep.

Friendships between women especially can be very affectionate. It wouldn't be unusual to see female friends walking down the street holding hands or with arms linked, which is rare among guy friends. Friendship groups can be mixed between men and women as you get older but there is more of a division between genders as young children, similar to probably how it is among young kids in the West.

Koreans, especially youth, love to party and celebrate. Drinking is one way to celebrate and Koreans love to drink. Men are expected to be able to hold their drink and not be a 'lightweight', while it would be expected for women to not drink as much. If a woman drinks quite a lot, many older Koreans would be critical of her, saying it's not lady-like for a woman to be publicly drunk and it would be considered more shameful than it is for a man to be drunk.

Social drinking takes place a lot after work, often with your boss. Depending on the specific culture of your workplace and the nature of your boss, it can be considered rude to refuse a drink from your boss. Generally, drinking is seen as a way of bonding and Koreans know how to drink and can hold their own. Many nights out can involve moving to multiple venues for a second, third and fourth round of drinking, referred to as *ee-cha* (이차), *sam-cha* (삼차) and *sah-cha* (사차), respectively.

Noreh bangs (노래방), which translates to 'song rooms', are karaoke bars and are another favourite activity in nightlife, as are nightclubs. Some of the best nightclubs are found in the Hongdae area of Seoul as well as the upscale area of the Gangnam District and most look and feel similar in terms of aesthetics to clubs in the West.

RIGHT: Lights outside lively bars and karaoke rooms in Seoul.

Other recreational activities

Shopping: as in many places around the world, shopping is a major pastime among Koreans and retail venues are always packed. Places to splurge in the capital, Seoul, range from the high-end shops in the Gangnam district to various markets including two major markets near Dongdaemun and Namdaemun, which are two of the Eight Great Gates that formed the Fortress Wall surrounding Seoul during the Joseon Dynasty. The four main gates include Dongdaemun (East Gate), Namdaemun (South Gate), Bukdaemun (North Gate) and Seodaemun (West Gate). The four smaller gates are also named after their location (Northwest, Northeast, Southwest and Southeast Gates). Of the eight gates, two no longer exist (the South and Southwest gates) as they were torn down during the Japanese occupation era.

There are several large shopping malls and department stores (Lotte, Dongdaemun Design Plaza and Coex Center Mall being among the most popular), as well as shopping centres underground alongside the metro system.

The shopping areas are dotted by rows of *muckjah golmoks*, which translates to 'let's eat streets' – slang or a nickname given to streets filled with many restaurants, stalls and other food venues. Food and shopping go hand-in-hand in South Korea.

Spectator sports: baseball and football are the top spectator sports in South Korea and people enjoy going to both games.

Baseball was first introduced to the country by American missionaries back in the 19th century (around 1896–1905) and in the 1920s players on tour from the American Major League stopped by the country to play an exhibition game against Koreans. The game was popular during the era of Japanese rule. Professional baseball teams in Korea were formed during the early 1980s and today there are 10 professional teams in the Korean Baseball Association, which is a member of the International Baseball Federation. Koreans have performed well on the international stage, scoring a gold medal in the sport during the 2008 Olympics in Beijing and a bronze medal during the 2000 Sydney Olympics, as well as twice ranking second place in the World Baseball Classic competition.

The country's Park Chan Ho paved the way for Korean baseball stardom in America when he went to play for the American Major League as a pitcher for the LA Dodgers in 1994. This was followed by a string of other successful Korean players being drafted into American baseball teams.

Football is another popular game followed avidly by sports fans in South Korea. Back in ancient times during the Silla dynasty, there was a form of football played that was called *chook, gook* (축국) – from where *chook goo* (축구), the Korean word for football originates. But the football we know today was first introduced to the country by crew members of a British vessel that visited the port of Incheon in around 1882. The country's love of the sport has grown since and it co-hosted the FIFA World Cup in 2002 with Japan, during which the South Korean national team (Taeguk Warriors) made it to the semifinals. The team has had eight FIFA World Cup finals appearances, making it one of the most successful Asian football teams in the world. Fans are super enthusiastic and can be seen following the national team everywhere for games, wearing face paint and matching red-themed shirts and other items, waving their flags and sometimes even bringing sets of hand drums to get each other pumped up to cheer for the team.

ABOVE: Team South Korea during their World Cup semi-final match against Germany on 25th June 2002 at Seoul World Cup Stadium.

At the Table

Food and drink, Korean style

From lip-smacking spicy street eats to innovative Michelin-starred fare, Korean cuisine has burst onto the culinary scenes of major capitals around the world in recent years, with the South Korean capital Seoul now boasting a Michelin Guide with more than 186 recommended venues, including nearly 30 Michelin-starred restaurants. Here, I'll take you through some of the basics of Korean dining etiquette, signature foods and how to navigate a Korean menu.

Humble beginnings

Before South Korea became the wealthy First World country it is today, Korean cuisine was simple and mostly vegetarian, with any form of meat being considered a luxury. Most of the country was historically a farming nation and, therefore, most of the country's diet consisted of homegrown vegetables and steamed rice, which continue to be an everyday staple.

Back in the day, barley, brown and wild rice were a staple and white rice was considered a luxury item that you would only find in wealthy households. In the modern era, it's now the opposite, as white rice is actually cheaper than barley and whole grain rice, which are both now considered the more expensive health-food options.

This simple and naturally healthier diet may explain why Koreans historically lived longer. The few farming communities in modern-day South Korea still have a healthier diet than those in urban areas, where there is a lot more processed foods available following the influence of the Western world.

How to eat

Before we tuck in, it's worth noting the basic dining style and structure of Korean cuisine. While most Western menus might offer dishes in the form of starters followed by mains, Korean food is neither as categorical nor sequential, though many Korean restaurants in English-speaking countries do group dishes according to this template. Korean menus offer larger dishes (which could be considered mains) and smaller side dishes known as *ban-chan* (반찬), but all are meant to be shared in a seated buffet style of eating.

RIGHT: Eating out with Korean barbecue dishes.

A typical Korean spread features several side dishes, such as *kimchee* (김치) – a quintessential Korean dish made with cabbage fermented in a spicy red pepper, chilli paste and fish sauce (we'll come back to this later) – and maybe a larger dish or two such as a casserole soup or cooked meat dish to be eaten with rice.

All things family are central to Korean culture and the same ethos can be seen in eating. In a typical Korean family home, everyone sits together around one table, each with their own bowl of rice, with lots of side dishes placed at the centre. Some families or singletons may not have space for a dining table and chairs and, therefore, many resort to just having a foldable small table that can be used for dining.

The traditional style of eating while sitting crossed-legged on the floor (sometimes on a floor cushion) still takes place around the country, especially in rural areas, but it also can be seen in urban homes. Of course it is more common in the poorer parts of the country, where families may not be able to afford a dining table or even a sofa, and therefore live very simply by eating over a small table while sitting on the floor. But many local restaurants across the country, from Seoul to rural parts of the country, still offer floor seating. And the practice of sitting on the floor isn't just reserved for dining, it's normal for family and friends to gather around and catch up while sitting on the floor of their living room as well.

ABOVE: **A variety of Korean side dishes.**

This shared dining practice can be traced back to the dynastic periods, when it was customary for even kings and queens to sit on the floor within their own private quarters and to eat or drink over a low table. The practice also stemmed from the post-war period of poverty, long before South Korea's economic boom, when families would have to survive sharing one main dish only. There's an old Korean adage that says slurping spoonfuls of soup from a shared hotpot is the best way of forming bonds with one another and this concept forms the basis of Korean dining culture.

Table manners and other rules around dining in Korea aren't complicated and not all are strictly enforced but the basic ones are generally linked to the concept of having respect for your elders. For example, if you are having a big family meal, you wouldn't begin eating until the oldest members of the family (such as the parents or grandparents) start eating, and it would be considered rude for you to pick up your spoon before any of the elders have picked up their spoon from the table. If the eldest person enters the room while you are dining, it would be rude to not get up out of your seat to properly greet them before you continue eating. These rules wouldn't apply if the person who enters the room is younger than you.

The average breakfast, lunch and dinner

Traditionally, there hasn't been much differentiation between the three meals in Korean cuisine, but in modern times people have started following Western-style breakfasts, having pastries with coffee or juice, or a sandwich for lunch. With this influence of Western culture, food options and meal preferences have evolved, so there are lots of Koreans who will have a burger or a salad for lunch or dinner and have a smoothie with eggs and toast for breakfast. But traditionally, Korean people have a warm, hearty meal at home for breakfast, consisting of rice alongside a bowl of soup and a spread of different side dishes, as you would for any other meal. Where possible, they would do the same for lunch and, of course, dinner – and this is still seen in many homes. It's also common for people to have a cup of coffee after meals, even if it's in the evening. Some traditional restaurants offer free coffee from a small self-service coffee machine that people can easily access.

How to drink

Similar to the manners required around eating, there is an etiquette for drinking when having an alcoholic drink with those that are older than you. When someone older than you pours you a drink, you should receive the drink with both hands rather than one, as a sign of respect. The same would apply for when you are pouring a drink for someone older than you – you should pour it while holding the bottle with both hands rather than one, as a gesture of respect for the elder person.

When you consume a drink offered to you by an older person, it's also respectful to drink it with your head turned to the side, rather than knocking the drink back while facing the elder person directly, as this is considered a sign of disrespect and arrogance. Some popular Korean alcoholic drinks include *soju* (소주), a clear distilled drink similar to Japanese *sake*, *maekju* (맥주) beer and *makgeolli* (막걸리), a rice wine with a milky look and slightly sweet and tangy taste. Among typical non-alcoholic drinks is *bori cha* (보리차), barley tea that can be served hot or cold, and *shik-hae* (식혜), a sweet, rice dessert drink containing soft, wilted grains of rice and garnished with pine nuts.

ABOVE: *Soju* is a popular Korean drink that is similar to Japanese *sake*.

How to navigate a Korean menu

With a mouth-wateringly dizzying array on offer, it's hard to know where the modern fusion fare ends and the authentic traditional dishes begin. For the purists out there, like myself, here are some of the most typical Korean dishes you'll see at a Korean restaurant.

Popular dishes

Kimchee (김치): as mentioned earlier, this is the most quintessential Korean staple you'll find in every Korean household. It is served with practically every meal as a standard side dish. There are a host of varieties of *kimchee* made with different types of vegetables, from *oheekimchee* (made with cucumbers) and *mookimchee* (radish kimchee) to *buchukimchee* (made with chives).

Bulgogi (불고기) and *galbi* (갈비): probably the most well-known Korean dishes among non-natives, *bulgogi* (which translates to 'fire meat') and *galbi* (ribs) are both Korean barbecue dishes. Both meats are soaked overnight in a sweet sesame oil and soy sauce marinade, then cooked over a barbecue fire. Both are eaten with steamed rice wrapped in *sangchoo* (a leaf of lettuce) and a dollop of *samjang* (a spicy soybean and red pepper paste) for each bite.

Pajeon (파전): a savoury pancake made with spring onions and a flour batter mix. There are several other types of *jeon* (전) usually on offer, including *kimchee jeon*, *haemul pajeon* (seafood scallion pancake) and *yahchae jeon* (vegetable pancake).

Samgyeopsalgui (삼겹살구이): grilled pork belly eaten either alongside rice and a spicy soup or casserole. It can also be eaten with spoonfuls of steamed rice wrapped in *sangchoo*, as with the *bulgogi* and *galbi* meats.

Soondooboo jjigae (순두부찌개): a *jjigae* (찌개) is a thick soup or casserole. This spicy *jjigae* is made with vegetables and soft tofu simmered in a red pepper powder-based stew. Served in a hot stone bowl, the soup is topped with a raw egg that cooks from the high temperature of the soup. It's eaten alongside a bowl of rice.

Bibimbap (비빔밥): a classic rice dish (*bibim* means 'mixing' or 'folding together'), featuring a mix of several sautéed vegetables as well as sautéed beef. It can be served cold or hot in a stone bowl topped with a fried egg and mixed with *gochujang* (고추장) – a spicy red pepper sauce. This dish is considered a main but is not a shared dish and rather served in individual portions.

Japchae (잡채): a warm glass noodle dish with mixed vegetables, mushrooms and beef sautéed in sesame oil and soy sauce, topped with strips of fried egg.

Yookgaejang (육개장): a spicy soup made with red pepper powder, sesame oil, beef, glass noodles and various vegetables like onions, peppers and chives. It's also eaten alongside a bowl of rice. This soup is a common hangover cure, with many preferring to have it just after a long night out to cleanse their system or wake them up after a night of excess alcohol.

Chimaek (치맥): the name of this dish comes from the word chicken and *maekju* (beer) combined. It is basically fried chicken, eaten while drinking *maekju*. People can also choose to have red-coloured spicy fried chicken (양념 통닭 – *yang nyum tong dak*, which literally means 'seasoned whole chicken' in Korean) instead of the plain fried chicken.

ABOVE: *Bibimbap* is a typical Korean rice dish made with beef and mixed vegetables.

Naengmyeon (냉면): this cold noodle dish (*naeng* means 'cold' and *myeon* means 'noodle') is made with chewy buckwheat noodles set in a clear meat broth, seasoned with an anchovy-based powder, a touch of vinegar and garnished with slices of cooked beef, boiled egg, Asian pear and cucumber. It's usually topped with ice cubes to keep it extra cool. It's primarily a summer dish but can be eaten year-round. Those who want a spicy kick should try the *bibimnaengmyun*, which is made with the same chewy noodles and garnishes minus the broth and instead mixed with *gochujang* and slices of *kimchee*.

Goongim (구운김): these super thin sheets of toasted dried seaweed are brushed in sesame oil and salt. You'll see them in Western markets these days and many people like to snack on them. But Koreans mostly eat them by wrapping them around spoonfuls of steamed rice.

Typical Korean–Chinese dishes

As with its history, Korean cuisine has links to China, evolving from southern Manchuria. In modern-day Korea, there are several staple Chinese dishes that are served at Korean restaurants, with some even specializing solely in the following typical Chinese dishes.

Ganpoonggi (깐풍기): battered and fried pieces of chicken or shrimp with a very spicy kick.

Jjajangmyeon (짜장면): a warm noodle dish consisting of thick, chewy noodles mixed with a black bean sauce made with sautéed onions and pieces of pork or seafood, including shrimp and squid. It's served with *dakgwang* (닥광), a bright yellow radish pickled in vinegar and *kimchee* as side dishes.

Jjamppong (짬뽕): a warm noodle soup consisting of the same thick and chewy noodles used to make the *jjajangmyeon* dish, but simmered in a hot and spicy broth made with sautéed vegetables including seaweed and different types of seafood such as shrimp, clams, oysters and squid.

Tangsuyook (탕수육): battered and fried pieces of beef covered in a clear sweet-and-sour sauce.

ABOVE: Customers at a Korean street-food stall at Gwangjang Market, Seoul.

Korean street food

The following foods can be found in various street-food markets as well as in a *pojangmacha* (포장마차), which literally translates to 'packaged cart'. These covered food stands can be found in back streets off the main roads in different cities across South Korea. They provide small plastic tables and seats and sell food and alcohol (usually *soju*). These aren't glamorous settings but are good for a quick, cheap and cheerful late-night bite or drink after work, with one or two friends or even by yourself.

Pojangmachas can be traced back to the 1950s and 1960s when people used to sell snacks from an open pushcart they wheeled up and down the road. With the emergence of modern restaurants, these mobile makeshift vendors faded out and were modified into *pojangmachas*, which are also dwindling. But they are the closest remaining vestiges of the pushcart tradition.

Ddukbokki **(떡볶이):** chewy rice cakes simmered in a spicy red pepper sauce made using *gochujang*, *gochugaru*, vegetable oil, garlic powder and a touch of sugar. Many modern versions also include noodles, slices of imitation crab meat sausages, fish cakes, potatoes and other vegetables in the mix.

Gimbap (김밥): similar to sushi, this seaweed wrap is made using steamed rice mixed with salt and sesame oil that is spread across a sheet of non-toasted dried seaweed. Then it's lined with thin layers of *bulgogi*, sesame oil-seasoned spinach, slices of cucumber, *dakgwang* and fried egg. There are many versions of *gimbap*, from spicy tuna to chicken, but beef is the traditional version.

Uh mook (어묵): these fish cakes are served on wooden sticks placed in a cup of hot fish broth that can be slurped to wash them down.

Boonguhbbang (붕어빵): warm fried bread, made in the shape of a goldfish, with a sweet, red-bean paste filling.

Five unusual Korean delicacies

Korean cuisine varies across the country and as a result, there are many unique delicacies beloved by some Koreans that many might find to be an acquired taste.

Nakjee (낙지): these are live octopi, served either in small pieces or as a whole octopus. In both cases, they're still squirming around on the plate as well as when they go down your throat, since you're meant to swallow them whole. They're often served soaked in sesame oil for seasoning but also to help prevent the suction cups on the octopus from sticking to your throat and mouth.

Bundaegi (번데기): these silkworm larvae are actually a street-food delicacy. Boiled and seasoned, they're served hot in small cups. It was a popular source of protein during the Korean War when many families were poor and food was scarce.

Soondae (순대): these black pig intestine sausages are steamed, stuffed with glass noodles, coagulated pig's blood and sometimes seafood or fish. It's a popular Korean street food.

Gaejang (게장): these are soft-shell crabs seasoned in various different spices and sauces. They're left to marinate in the sauces before they are consumed raw.

Dotorimook (도토리묵): this brown jelly-like substance is made from acorns, which are abundant in Korea. The acorns are cooked to remove their toxins and made into jelly form. They're usually served as a side dish, seasoned with soy sauce and a sprinkling of red pepper powder and topped with vegetable garnishes. Despite the unusual texture, it has a pleasant, nutty taste.

Korean cupboard staples

If you delve into any Korean household cupboard, you're likely to come across some of the following food staples and ingredients.

Bap (밥): steamed rice is the bread and butter of all Korean meals. It is usually cooked in a rice cooker in most homes these days but used to be cooked in stone pots during historic times. In many restaurants and homes, the rice is served in a metal or ceramic bowl that comes with its own cover to keep it warm.

Ganjang (간장): soy sauce, a staple in many Asian households, which originated in Korea during the Koguryo era (2nd century BC to 668 AD). Korea was the first to introduce soybean fermentation, which sparked the soy sauce culture across the Orient, and Koreans began teaching neighbouring countries how to ferment soybeans. Soy sauce, as well as *dwenjang* (more on this paste below), have been used in Korea for around 2,000 years and form the base of Korean cuisine.

Dooboo (두부): another ingredient made from soybeans, this is tofu. It used in a host of soups, casseroles and stir-fries or it can also be eaten raw.

Dwenjang (된장): this salty paste made from soybeans is often compared to Japan's miso, for its similar colour, texture and taste. This paste has been a staple in the country for many years; it's still preserved in large ceramic barrels in many rural areas and even in urban households. Its saltiness has allowed it to be stored outdoors without fear of it spoiling. Soybeans were traditionally a key ingredient in so many Korean foods because they were the easiest and cheapest bean to grow, so many resourceful Korean farmers made use of it in many different ways.

Gochugaru (고추가루): this is ground red chili pepper powder, which you'll see sold in large packets in every Korean food shop. It comes in fine- and coarse-ground forms. This spicy ingredient is used in a variety of Korean dishes to give it a spicy kick in taste and in colour.

Gochujang (고추장): this red chili pepper paste is made from a mix of *gochugaru*, soybeans and flour. *Gochujang* is often stored outdoors in large ceramic barrels in farming communities.

Chamgeerum (참기름): this is sesame oil, another staple used in several Korean soups, casseroles, stir fries, marinades and more.

Dashida (다시다): this ground powder comes in either anchovy or beef flavour and is used to season various dishes, from Korean soups and casseroles to marinades.

ABOVE: Gochujang and Gochugaru.

Baechoo (배추): this Korean cabbage is similar in appearance to the Chinese bok choy but much larger in size. It is the vegetable used to make *kimchee* but is also used in soups and casseroles.

Moo (무): this radish is different from the smaller red radishes seen in Western markets. These white radishes are much bigger and therefore heavier as well. *Moo* is used in several Korean soups and side dishes.

Kongnamul (콩나물): these are bean sprouts, which are staple vegetables used in lots of Korean soups, as well as side dishes.

Hobak (호박): Grey squash is another vegetable used in several Korean soups, stir-fries and savoury pancakes. It's much larger in diameter and lighter in colour than the darker, skinnier courgettes seen in Western markets.

Staple Korean recipes

Here are some typical dishes that you might encounter on a table spread in a Korean home, which are simple to make using just a handful of standard Korean ingredients. Some of these dishes require mixing ingredients with your own two hands, which Koreans call *sohn maht* (손맛), which translates to 'handmade taste'. It refers to the devotion behind Korean cooking, which they believe is the key ingredient that makes a good tasty dish.

Bear in mind that traditionally, cooking in Korean culture isn't an exact science, in the way that baking or other types of cooking might be in many Western cultures. So the recipes and ingredient listings below are general guidelines and can be adjusted according to taste preference, be it adding more or less sugar or salt, chili or garlic, etc.

Oheemoochim (오이무침)

This is a spicy cucumber side dish which requires no cooking, just chopping and mixing together of the ingredients.

Ingredients:
1 large cucumber
2 small garlic cloves
½ thin scallion (spring onion)
½ tbsp of dashida powder
1 tbsp of gochugaru

Serves 2

Cut the cucumber into thin slices and place into a large mixing bowl.

Add the *dashida*, a tablespoon of *gochugaru* (add less *gochugaru*, if you don't want it too spicy), the smashed garlic and thin slices of fresh-cut scallions.

Use your hands (with plastic gloves, if preferred) to mix the vegetables together to evenly distribute the seasoning.

Serve at room temperature as a side dish.

Dwenjang jjigae (된장찌개)

This hearty, thick soup is made with a *dwenjang* base (see page 173) and *dooboo* (tofu), as well as different vegetables including *hobak* (grey squash), potatoes, peppers, scallions (spring onion), onions and garlic. It's traditionally a non-spicy dish, but I like to add red chilli pepper powder to give it a spicy kick. It's eaten alongside a bowl of rice.

Ingredients:

2 tbsp of dwenjang
½ tbsp of gochugaru (optional)
½ tbsp of dashida powder
2 small garlic cloves
2 small potatoes
1 small onion
1 or 2 skinny green or red chili peppers (optional)
1 small hobak (grey squash)
1 packet of dooboo (tofu)
1 thin scallion (spring onion)

Serves 2

Place the *dwenjang* into a small pot of water over medium heat. Loosen the paste with a spoon and add the *gochugaru*, if you fancy a spicy version of this dish. Add the *dashida* powder into the mix.

Smash the garlic cloves and throw into the pot. Chop up the potatoes and onion in fairly chunky but even pieces and then add into the pot.

Slice the green or red chili peppers (you can skip this if you don't want the soup to be too spicy), add to the pot and let it all simmer together for a few minutes.

Chop up the *hobak* into chunky, half-circle slices and add to the mix.

Cut the *dooboo* into chunky, rectangular slices and slowly add to the pot. Let it simmer for approximately 10–15 minutes, until the potatoes and other vegetables are nearly cooked.

Once the vegetables seem cooked, add some slices of scallion to the top of the soup, cover the pot and simmer for another 5 minutes or so, just enough for the scallions to slightly wither.

Serve with a bowl of steamed rice.

Kimchee jjigae (김치찌개)

This is a simple spicy casserole/soup made using *kimchee*, sesame oil, onions, garlic, with some *gochugaru* (see page 173) and *dashida* powder (see page 174). It's a great way to get rid of any *kimchee* that's been fermenting away for a while (익은 김치, which translates to 'ripe kimchee') in your fridge. But it can be made using *kimchee* at any stage.

Ingredients:
½ tbsp of dashida powder
½ tbsp of gochugaru
2 small garlic cloves
½ small onion
1 tsp of sesame oil
½ cup [approx. 4oz/110g]
    of kimchee
2–3 tsp of sugar

Serves 2

Boil water in a small pot over medium heat. Add the *dashida* and *gochugaru* (add more or less according to how spicy you like it).

Smash the garlic cloves and cut the onion into half-circle slices. Add both the garlic and onion to the pot.

Pour in the sesame oil.

Slice your *kimchee* into square pieces (if it's not already been sliced when you bought it) and add to the pot. Add the sugar, then close the lid and let it simmer together for a while, approximately 15 minutes or so, until the *kimchee* is semi-soft and wilted (the *kimchee* should appear almost translucent). It should taste quite savoury and spicy with a sweet touch.

Serve with a bowl of steamed rice.

Kongnamul gook (콩나물국)

This spicy beansprout soup is commonly described by Koreans to be a *shee won han* (시원한) – 'refreshing' dish to have as a hangover cure or to help fight a cold. It just requires beansprouts, *gochugaru* (see page 173), *dashida* powder (see page 174), garlic and onions.

Ingredients:
1 cup [approx. 7oz/200g]
    kongnamul (beansprouts)
1 tbsp of dashida powder
3–4 tbsp of gochugaru
1 small onion
1 thin scallion (spring onion)
2 small garlic cloves, smashed
1 tsp of salt

Serves 2

Cut the root tips off the beansprouts. Add to a small pot over a medium heat.

Add the *dashida*, salt and the *gochugaru* (add one more or less tablespoon of *gochugaru*, depending on how spicy you like it).

Cut the onion into thin slices and add to the pot, along with the smashed garlic.

Cover with a lid and let it simmer for approximately 20 minutes or so, until the beansprouts are cooked (they should look wilted and translucent).

Serve with a bowl of rice.

Kongnamul moochim (콩나물무침)

This easy side dish is made with steamed beansprouts tossed in sesame oil, smashed garlic, *dashida* powder (see page 174) and scallions. This dish can also be made using steamed spinach instead of beansprouts.

Ingredients:
1 cup [approx. 7oz/200g]
    kongnamul (beansprouts)
1 tsp of sesame oil
½ tbsp of dashida powder
2 small garlic cloves
½ thin scallion (spring onion)
1 tsp of salt

Serves 2

Cut the root tips off the beansprouts. Steam the beansprouts or a few handfuls of spinach, if using instead.

Place the steamed beansprouts or spinach into a large bowl. Add the sesame oil, the *dashida*, salt, two smashed garlic cloves and thin slices of the fresh-cut scallion into the mix.

Using plastic gloves or your bare hands, mix the vegetables together to evenly distribute the seasoning.

Serve at room temperature as a side dish.

Korean ramyeon (라면)

Koreans love eating instant noodles, especially the spicy kind. Many people have it as a quick lunch or even as a late-night bite, and usually have it with a side of *kimchee*. Some of the most popular classic Korean *ramyeon* brands include *Neoguri* (너구리), *Shin Ramyeon* (신라면) and more recently the *Buldak Bokkeum Myeon* (불닭볶음면, which literally means 'fire chicken fried noodle'), which is a super-spicy chicken flavoured instant noodle that is seriously hot and not for the faint-hearted. Koreans like to jazz up their instant noodle dishes (the ones you cook in the pot, as opposed to the ones that come in a cup) to make it heartier and more satisfying. Here's one way I like to make my Korean instant noodles.

Ingredients:

1 packet of ramyeon (any of the
    Korean ones I mentioned above
    will do)
½ small onion
½ small hobak (grey squash)
1–2 eggs
½ thin scallion (spring onion)
1 tsp of gochujang

Serves 1

Add the spicy soup mix from the instant noodle packet to a small pot of water.

Cut the onion into thin, half-circle slices. Cut the *hobak* into thin, julienne-style strips. Add both vegetables to the pot.

Add the noodles to the pot and cook for 5 minutes, or until they're slightly soft.

Crack one or two eggs into a bowl and pour the eggs into the pot as the soup simmers.

Add thin slices of scallion to the top of the mix. Close the lid and let it simmer for a minute or two until the eggs are cooked.

For an extra kick, you can add a teaspoon of *gochujang* (but skip this if you don't want it too spicy).

Enjoy with a side dish of *kimchee*.

K Culture

A brief history of K-pop

While the K-pop music genre began to rise in the early 1990s, it was the success of the song 'Gangnam Style' by South Korean rapper Psy that turned it into the global phenomenon it has become today. As a fellow Korean, seeing Psy's now famous horse-riding dance move featured on television screens across the world, a good part of me cringed in embarrassment for it being so cheesy. Yet the world embraced the tune and danced with open arms, igniting strong interest in K-pop from a Western audience for the first time.

K-pop music first took off around 1992, featuring a hybrid of elements borrowed from other genres including pop, rock, hip-hop, R&B and electronic music, with one of the earliest K-pop groups being Seo Taiji and Boys (서태지와 아이들). This influential band was the first-ever to incorporate rap into Korean songs, which shifted the Korean music industry. A few major K-pop stars of this era went on to launch music labels that have become major players today, such as JYP Entertainment, created by Park Jin Young (also known as J.Y. Park), which has produced some of the most popular K-pop artists in the country. Singer-songwriter Park was a big K-pop star back in the day but today is a major music executive and producer at his own label.

Some of the first popular K-pop acts included boy bands H.O.T. and DJ DOC and girl groups S.E.S. and Fin.K.L. They all thrived in Korea in the 1990s, along with countless others who I grew up listening to, but are now considered veterans of K-pop. DJ DOC were particularly known for their rebel image, at times using profanity and criticising social injustices in their music. They became one the first K-pop groups in the country whose songs were censored because of their controversial lyrics.

By the 2000s, K-pop became a bona fide term in the music industry and a cultural phenomenon complete with its own fashion and style trends. Twenty years on, its influence remains global with several big name international artists such as Kanye West, Snoop Dogg and Ludacris having been featured in some K-pop songs. K-pop music has become a global ambassador for South Korea in recent years and a gateway for foreigners to explore other aspects of Korean culture in a bid to better understand the music itself.

In January 2020, the country's King Sejong Institute, named after the fourth king of the Joseon Dynasty (1392–1910) who created the Korean language *hangul* (한글), which offers Korean language programmes around the world, announced it would be introducing 30 new institutes across Southeast Asia,

Russia, Africa, Central and South America in the coming years to accommodate the increase in demand for learning the Korean language because of the influence of K-pop. Fans of the seven-member K-pop boy band BTS – collectively known as the Army – have shown a desire to learn the language in order to better understand the Korean lyrics to their songs but also to be able to better communicate with and understand the band themselves.

The King Sejong Institute said it currently offers 180 different Korean language institutions across 60 countries and the government's Ministry of Culture, Sports and Tourism has put 33.2 billion South Korean won towards the institute's global expansion.

Five key K-pop artists

There have been a number of history-making K-pop artists in recent years that have created key defining moments of the genre and its evolution. Here are five of the most significant.

Psy: as mentioned, this solo artist took the international stage by storm with the release of his song 'Gangnam Style' which put K-pop on the musical landscape of the world for the first time, igniting a unique wave of interest in

ABOVE: 'Gangnam Style' star Psy poses at a press conference before a concert in Seoul.

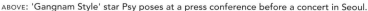

K-pop and Korean culture on a global scale. In December 2012, Psy's video for 'Gangnam Style' was reported to be the first-ever video on YouTube to reach a billion views, less than six months after it was released in July 2012. The song has since been watched more than 3.4 billion times. In 2019, he started his own music label P Nation and has been signing other K-pop stars.

Monsta X: this South Korean boy-band debuted in 2015 and has released songs in Korean, English and Japanese, which has heightened their global success. They shot to international fame following their appearances on major television programmes in the US, including *Good Morning America*, *Jimmy Kimmel Live* and *The Ellen DeGeneres Show*. The group's string of English singles has made it easier for the US audience to embrace the band's music. Monsta X was the first K-pop group to perform at a major music festival in the US with their appearance at the *Life is Beautiful Music & Art Festival* in Las Vegas in 2018. In the same year, they were the first K-pop headline act at the major *Jingle Ball* concert series in America.

These music festival appearances paid off because by 2019, Monsta X was signed by Columbia Records UK, the major record label behind some of the biggest names in music, from artists including Calvin Harris, Harry Styles, Mark Ronson, Kings of Leon and Foo Fighters to music legends including Bob Dylan, Leonard Cohen, Bruce Springsteen and AC/DC, among a host of others. Later that year, the band was subsequently signed by Epic Records, the major American label who have previously released music from legends including Michael Jackson and Mariah Carey, and more recently from Camilla Cabello.

They've caught the eye of big name artists such as will.i.am, Pitbull and French Montana, all of whom have released songs with the band. In early 2020, they released their first all-English-language album and their many English tracks have given them an edge in terms of connecting lyrically with their audience, and certainly given them great worldwide success.

Blackpink: this four-piece girl band has been rising to the top of the K-pop girl-group music scene in recent years. They made history in 2019 with the music video of their 2018 song, '뚜두뚜두 (DDU-DU DDU-DU)', which received a billions views, becoming the most-viewed video by a K-pop group on YouTube.

ABOVE LEFT: Four-piece girl group Blackpink performing on *The Late Late Show with James Corden* in 2019.
BELOW LEFT: The six members of MonstaX – Shownu, I.M, Minhyuk, Joohoney, Kihyun and Hyungwon.

They were also reported to be the most subscribed music group on the video sharing website, as of September 2019.

Blackpink swept the rankings at last year's People's Choice Awards, usurping BTS in the categories for best Group, Music Video and Concert Tour of 2019. Part of their success may be in the diversity of the group, which includes Thai member Lisa and Rosé, who is a New Zealand–Korean singer who was born in Auckland to South Korean immigrant parents, while the other two members Jisoo and Jennie are South Koreans born and raised in Korea. Their mixed background helps them stand out from other K-pop girl groups and opens up a wider audience of people from other countries.

The group has only been on the scene since 2016, but as of 2019 they were reported to be the highest-charting female K-pop act on the *Billboard Hot 100* and *Billboard 200* charts.

BTS: some of the recent triumphs of this boy-band sensation include becoming the first Korean act to perform at the Grammy Awards, the biggest night in the global music industry, in 2020. They performed the song 'Seoul Town Road' with Lil Nas X, which is a remix of the song 'Old Town Road' released by the American rapper/singer-songwriter. This was the band's second appearance at the awards – in 2019, they were presenters of the Grammy Award for the best R&B album of the year.

In the same month, the band also became the first Korean act to have a platinum album in the US, with their 2018 record *Love Yourself: Answer*. That same album had already become the first K-pop album to spend a year on the Billboard 200 album chart in April 2019.

The group has received several nods of recognition in Europe, including at the 2019 MTV European Music Awards, where they won awards for Best Group and Best Live Act, while other big name acts such as Ariana Grande and their recent collaborator Lil Nas X were nominated but walked away empty handed.

Girls' Generation: this K-pop girl band, also known as SNSD (which is short for *Sonyeo Sidae*, meaning 'girl generation' in Korean), made their official debut in 2007. But their fame began after 2009 with the release of their song 'Gee.'

They've often been called 'The Spice Girls of Korea,' although not from a musical standpoint but for their status as a national treasure. They were the first K-pop girl group to get noticed by Western media after winning Best Video of the Year at the inaugural YouTube Awards in 2013, usurping a powerhouse of other pop stars nominated in the same category, including Justin Bieber, Lady Gaga and their compatriot Psy. It took some time before Western audiences warmed up to the group but they can be credited for igniting the now thriving Korean Wave. The English version of their song 'The Boys' peaked at No. 5 on the *Billboard* music chart Hot Dance Singles in the US, making them among the first K-pop girl groups to chart on *Billboard*. They also became the first girl group to have three videos with more than 100-million views of each on YouTube, surpassing the record of two videos by The Pussycat Dolls.

They performed on *The David Letterman Show* in 2012, becoming the first-ever K-pop girl group to perform on a prime time evening TV show, and their song 'I Got a Boy' was recently chosen among the songs that defined the decade by *Billboard* in 2019.

Korean fan culture

Celebrity cult status and fan culture is very unique to Korea. Fans are incredibly obsessive over K-pop stars and other celebrities. K-pop stars often hold meet and greet events where fans can chat with their favourite idols. At such events, it wouldn't be unusual for idols to hold fans' hands while chatting to them and signing their albums. Reputation is very important for celebrity popularity in Korea and fan reaction can make or break a career. For this reason, many K-pop stars hide their relationship status, or in some cases remain single by order of their management companies, to avoid upsetting any passionate fans.

In 2020, the K-pop singer Chen, a member of K-pop boy-band EXO, unveiled he was getting married to his unexpectedly pregnant girlfriend. He has received a lot of backlash from fans who have been devastated and took the news very personally. Back in 2019, fans gathered in protest for months outside Starship Entertainment after the music label announced Wonho from its band Monsta X would be departing the group, demanding his reinstatement. So, Korean fans don't mess about.

But why is this the case? It partly has to do with the fact that many Korean kids feel repressed from a young age, bound by a rigorous schedule of studies with not much free time, banned from pursuing relationships until they are much older. So, they idolize these celebrity figures and are extremely protective of them, developing almost a personal relationship with them. Therefore, extreme jealousy and disappointment ensues when their favourite singer or actor is found to be dating or getting married.

Korean cinema

Korean cinema, which celebrated its 100th year in 2019, has certainly been having its moment in recent months, with several films starting to get international recognition and Hollywood buzz. Most recently, *Parasite*, directed by Bong Joon Ho, won four of the six categories for which the film was nominated at the 2020 Academy Awards, including the top prize of Best Picture. Bong has clearly paved the way for budding Korean filmmakers in Hollywood and piqued the interest of film lovers all over the world to discover more of the Korean cinema landscape. Here are some of the most groundbreaking and recognized classic South Korean films any movie buff should see.

Top 5 Korean movies you need to see

Parasite: Bong's 2019 black-comedy thriller explores themes around the perils of poverty and class disparities, as father Kim Ki Taek (played by Song Kang Ho) and his family begin working for the wealthy Park family. The story gets darker through a series of surprising twists as well as comic turns that lead to a haunting end. *Parasite* is just one of the Hollywood films Bong has released in recent years, such as *Okja* (starring Tilda Swinton, Jake Gyllenhaal and Paul Dano, which was also nominated for the Palme d'Or Award at the 2017 Cannes Film Festival) and *Snowpiercer* (a 2013 film starring Tilda Swinton, Chris Evans, Jamie Bell, Octavia Spencer and Ed Harris).

The Handmaiden: paving the way for the success of *Parasite*, fellow renowned South Korean director Park Chan Wook's *The Handmaiden* won the 2018 BAFTA

LEFT: Park So Dam as Kim Ki Jung and Choi Woo Shik as Kim Ki Woo in the 2019 film *Parasite*.

The road to the Oscars

Parasite is the first-ever foreign film to win the Best Picture category in the 92-year-history of the Academy Awards. Its other big wins of the night included Best Director, Best Original Screenplay and Best International Feature Film. Not a bad start for a first-time Oscar-nominated director and Korean film.

The film bagged some historic wins throughout 2019–2020, starting with the Palme d'Or Award at the 2019 Cannes Film Festival, becoming the first South Korean film to win by a unanimous vote. The film was critically acclaimed as the best South Korean film ever made and one of the best films of the decade.

Running on the energy from Cannes, in 2020 the film scored a Screen Actors Guild Award (winning the award for Outstanding Performance by a Cast in Motion Picture) and became the first non-English film to win this SAG category. In the same year, the film was also nominated for four BAFTA Awards and won both the Best Film Not in the English Language and Best Original Screenplay categories.

for Best Foreign Language Film. The film is based on a book by Welsh writer Sarah Waters, with its setting switched from Victorian Britain to Korea during the era of Japanese occupation. The psychological erotic thriller is a dark tale of love, betrayal and deception that unfolds between con artist Count Fujiwara, Japanese heiress Hideko, her maid Sook Hee and her uncle Kouzuki. The gripping unusual story was the highest grossing foreign-language film in the UK in 2017.

The Host: Bong's 2006 film was one of the first big-budget Hollywood blockbuster-style monster movies in South Korea but it managed to be so without losing its Korean spirit, with a storyline that centres around a sea creature found in the Han River in Seoul. The plot was inspired partially by a real-life incident that took place in 2000, when a Korean undertaker working at

ABOVE RIGHT: Film still from Park Chan Wook's 2016 film *The Handmaiden*.
BELOW RIGHT: Film still from Bong Joon Ho's 2006 film *The Host*.

a US military base in Seoul was reportedly told to pour large amounts of formaldehyde down a drain. This raised environmental concerns and anti-US sentiment at the time, so there's a slight political message to the film. It was one of the only South Korean films that was said to have been praised by North Korea because of its anti-American message, however slight it might have been. It was also reportedly one of Quentin Tarantino's 20 favorite films since 1992, the year he began his career as an independent filmmaker.

Oldboy: released in 2003, this thriller is one of director Park Chan Wook's most famous films and one of the most well-known Korean cinematic works outside its native country. It caught the eye of Hollywood in 2013 when acclaimed filmmaker Spike Lee released an American remake of it starring Samuel L. Jackson and Josh Brolin. Both films are based on the Japanese manga book *Old Boy* by Garon Tsuchiya. It's a bit of *Matrix* meets *Memento* with a *Kill Bill* feel, following the story of Oh Dae Su (played by Choi Min Sik, an award-winning legendary South Korean actor) who wakes up in a prison that looks like a hotel room and sets out on a quest for vengeance and answers to find out who and what got him there. *Oldboy* is actually the second part of a three-part trilogy by Park known as *The Vengeance Trilogy*.

Joint Security Area: this 2000 film, also by Park, stars *Parasite* actor Song Kang Ho and Lee Byung Hun (another one of South Korea's biggest film stars who made it to Hollywood with a string of films including the *G.I. Joe* film series and *The Magnificent Seven*). Set in the DMZ, the film sees four soldiers (two from the South and two from the North) on border duties form a genuine bond by chance after a shared near-death experience, agreeing to put aside politics in their friendship. But an unexpected turn of events causes their loyalty to be in question and tension unfolds. Though it is based on a fictional novel called *DMZ*, the film paints a realistic picture of what could potentially happen between soldiers at the border, as well as the complex relationship between North and South Korea beyond a political level.

Television

Korean television dramas are big business across Asia and watching these dramas is one of the most popular leisure activities in the country across all age groups. Many viewers follow these dramas just as fervently as they do K-pop, so the cult status is virtually the same for the stars of both industries.

While Korean TV dramas haven't really taken off in the Western media – at least not yet – anyone who wants to learn more about Korean culture would certainly appreciate the hype around Korean dramas and their importance to the country's culture.

I've grown up watching several different series, from historical to rom-coms, with my family at different periods of my life. What I've found interesting across them all is how you can basically start watching any show at any point in the series and you're able to catch up on the storyline and still enjoy it as if you'd been following it all along.

Many do offer a faint glimpse of what life in Korea is like from the inside, even if it might be a highly idealized version with extremely polished looking, well-put together characters. It can offer some insight on current trends in fashion and other industries.

Listed below are some Korean dramas series that had a cult following in the country and could be worth exploring.

Feelings (*Neukkim*, 느낌): this mid-1990s television series was especially popular because of its star-studded cast featuring multiple young Korean celebrities, many of whose careers took off after appearing on this series. The series follows a group of university friends who get caught up in love triangles and other dramatic situations.

The Hourglass (*Moreh-shigae*, 모래시계): this mid-1990s historical drama became one of Korea's highest-rated TV series in history and follows the story of three friends during the country's period of political turmoil in the 1970s and 1980s in a gripping melodramatic tale of love, loyalty and oppression. Incorporating real archival footage from the historical period, it was deemed one of the most realistic portrayals in Korean television history at the time.

ABOVE: *Graceful Family* is one of the latest Korean dramas to capture a large audience.

Autumn Tale (*Gah-ul-dongha*, **가을동화**): this drama series from 2000 is a dramatic tale of love, loss and tragedy that takes place between two men who fall in love with the same woman. The series was incredibly successful and is said to have first launched the Korean Wave fever. The country launched several tourist sites relating to the show following its popularity.

Vagabond (**배가본드**): this action thriller series, which aired in late 2019, is one among the more than 200 recent Korean drama series now available for viewing on Netflix. It offers a mix of the US television series *Homeland* and *Lost*, following the story of a Korean national intelligence agent and civilian who uncover the political corruption and government conspiracies surrounding a mysterious plane crash that kills hundreds and is linked to terrorists. The action series is a definite detour from the more typical dramatic love story or romantic comedy feel of many Korean dramas series.

Graceful Family (**우아한 가**): this melodrama mystery series, which also aired in late 2019, follows the story of a troubled young daughter of a wealthy *chaebol* family who is shunned by her father and stepmother following the death of her biological mother. She is sent to live and study in the US after her mother dies, but returns to South Korea 15 years later as a grown woman and uncovers some dark secrets about her family's past. In many ways it combines all the typical elements of a Korean drama including romance, comedy and a tragic backstory from the past, but also touches on prevailing class differences in Korean society. The series had the highest rating ever in the history of its television network MBN, a major South Korean cable network, and international success, sold to broadcasters in Asia as well as North and South America.

Art and design

The Korean contemporary art scene has been riding the Korean Wave and the appetite for it has been growing from both outside and within the country. In the past five or so years, a unique form of Korean monochromatic painting known as *Dansaekhwa* (단색화), launched by a group of painters in Korea in the 1970s, has made a sudden resurgence in the global art world. It began gaining attention from major art institutions such as the Museum of Modern Art in New York, which welcomed *Conjunction 74-26* by octogenarian *Dansaekhwa* artist Ha Chong Hyun, into its permanent collection in 2015. Ha held his first-ever solo show in four decades in the Big Apple that year.

There is plenty more contemporary art to be explored in South Korea. Seoul is home to more than 100 galleries and museums such as the National Museum of Modern and Contemporary Art Korea (MMCA), which welcomes around 2.8 million visitors a year across its four campuses across the country.

Seoul's Leeum Samsung Museum of Art is a good place to get a taste of both Korean traditional art as well as contemporary art across its two sections, including works by Choi Jeong Hwa, a famed South Korean artist known for

ABOVE: Sculptures at the Leeum Samsung Museum of Art in Seoul.

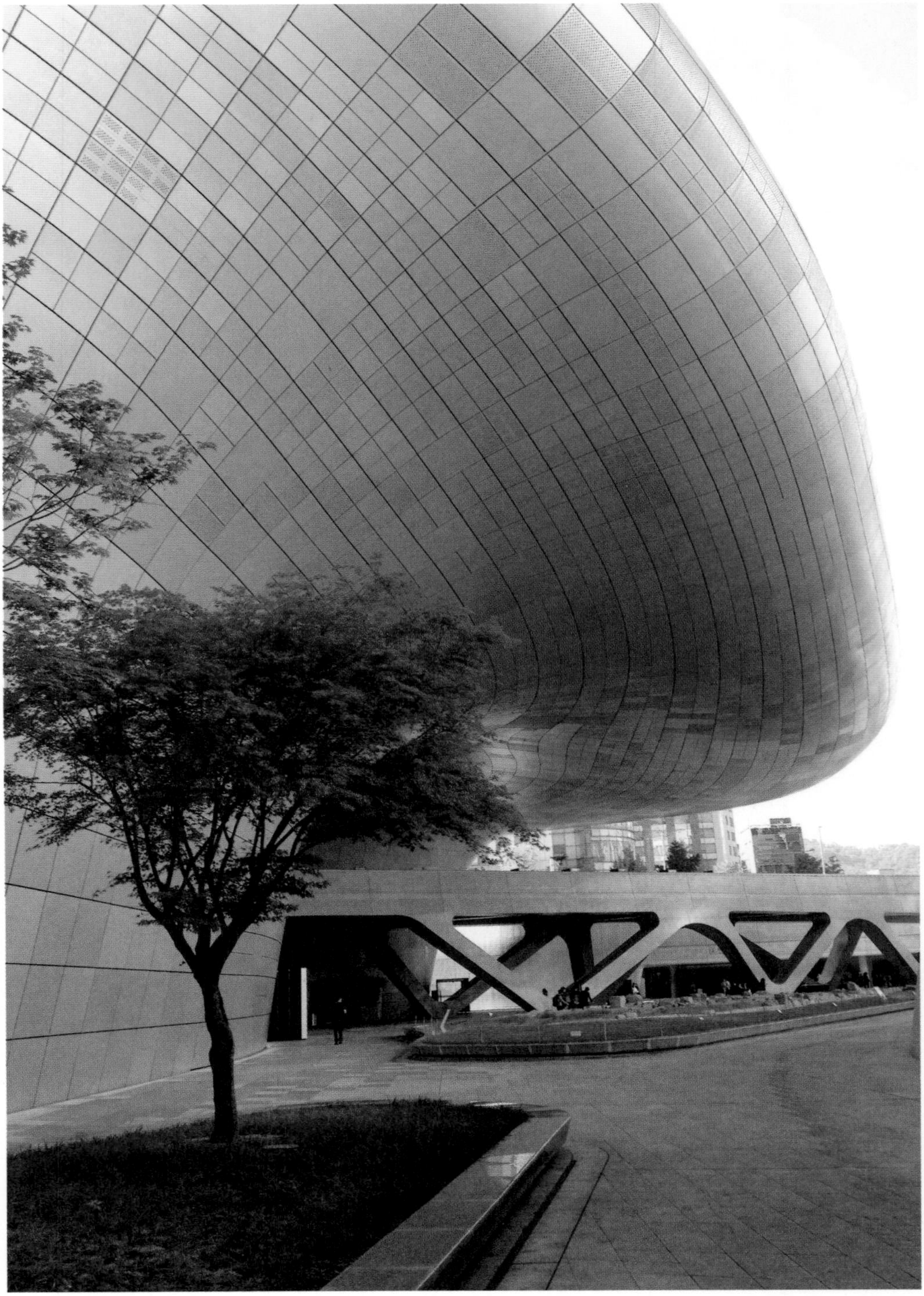

large-scale sculptures and installations that combine visual art, graphic and industrial design as well as architecture. Back in 2005, his work 'White Lotus', a giant flower made with inflatable polystyrene, was showcased at the Venice Biennale. Gwon Osang, also featured at the museum, is a South Korean artist who burst onto the contemporary art scene with his unique blend of photography and sculptural work, which entails covering life-sized sculptures with photographs. His pieces have been displayed in exhibitions and auctions around the world, including at Christie's in London.

The Leeum Samsung Museum of Art also houses permanent exhibition spaces for the works of world-renowned artists including Damien Hirst and Andy Warhol. Back in March 2019, acclaimed British artist David Hockney hosted his first-ever retrospective in South Korea at the Seoul Museum of Art, the artist's first large-scale solo exhibition in Asia.

The Gwangju Biennale in the city of Gwangju in the Jeollanamdo province is Asia's oldest biennale of contemporary art. Established in 1995 and held every two years, it was founded in memory of the Gwangju Uprisings in May 1980, which saw the death of thousands of civilians following the government's suppression of demonstrations against the military regime at the time. The art festival aims to nurture the area's cultural heritage as well as pay tribute and heal its tragic history through the expression of art.

For more design and art inspiration, the Dongdaemun Design Plaza is a must-see. Designed by the late British architect Zaha Hadid, the building is an artwork in itself featuring some of Hadid's signature futuristic silhouettes of undulating curves. The giant complex forms the centrepiece of the capital's bustling fashion district, with its spaceship-like structure and metallic facade lit up by night. This sprawling complex includes three underground and four above-ground levels with various public areas and art spaces including an exhibition hall and design museum.

Among other impressive modern structures of architectural interest in the capital is the Lotte World Tower. Standing 1,823 feet-high (555m) with 123 floors, it is the tallest building in South Korea and the fifth tallest in the world, as of 2020. Its cone-shaped structure and exterior design has been compared to The Shard in London. Its pale-coloured glass facade was inspired by Korean ceramics, which feature similar jade-like shades.

LEFT: A view of the futuristic Dongdaemun Design Plaza building in Seoul.

K CULTURE

197

Technology

In the opening scene of the film *Parasite*, the children of Kim Ki Taek, who live with their father in a cramped *banjiha* (반지하) – half-basement level house – walk around their home in an attempt to connect to their patchy Wi-Fi. While this poor family might have not had any food on the table, they still had smartphones. This unassuming scene depicts how essential and accessible the internet and technology is to everyone in South Korea, not just the wealthier upper classes.

In 2017, there were reportedly around 43.94 million internet users in South Korea, nearly 40.18 million of whom were mobile internet users. The country's current population is around 51.8 million and as of 2019, about 95.9 percent of it reportedly use the internet. The total number of internet users is projected to reach 45.02 million by 2021.

With such an increasingly high demand for internet usage, it's no surprise that in April 2019, the country became the first in the world to offer a nationwide 5G service, which reportedly allows a million electronic devices within a single square-kilometre zone to connect to the internet simultaneously. Users of the 5G network are said to be able to download entire films in less than a second.

Innovation in mobile phone technology has been one of South Korea's strengths for years and in 2019, Samsung unveiled its Galaxy Fold phone, which has a foldable screen made with a flexible polymer material. It allows the phone to be used like a small tablet, as needed, by opening and closing the screen like a book. The unique feature was one of the most groundbreaking technologies introduced to the mobile phone industry.

Part of the reason for the country's thriving technology industry is that at its heart, Koreans are driven by the desire to make a better, more convenient life for themselves, for which technology has served the country well, even back in the 1960s when rapid industrialization ushered the country into the modern age. The technology industry is not just driven by the desire for global domination in different fields, but is also very much about improving lives with technology, be it through creating new jobs for the industry or the use of the technology itself.

RIGHT: A guide robot and a cleaning robot roam through travellers at the departure lobby of Incheon airport.

Everyone, from millennials to the older generation, has embraced the benefits of technology, from using the many readily available self-order kiosks at fast-food chains to old Korean ladies ditching the old-fashioned pushcart for a motorized refrigerator cart to sell bottles of Yakult (the fermented skimmed milk drink that's been regularly consumed in Korea for decades). These cutting-edge carts are used to store the Yakult, as well as travel down the streets.

South Korea is also reportedly one of the world's largest implementers of automation, having the highest density of robots at 710 per 10,000 workers, which is significantly higher than the global average of around 85 per 10,000 workers. One of its latest innovations in automation has been robot baristas, which were introduced at various shopping malls, schools and corporate dining facilities in 2019. These robot baristas, which are essentially small coffee booths with a robotic arm at its centre, are said to be able to brew around 90 cups of coffee an hour and nearly 300 cups a day on a single charge of beans and supplies. The robots help cater to a large number of people more efficiently during peak dining times.

From July 2017, South Korean electronics giant LG introduced *Star Wars*-style R2-D2-like airport guide robots at Incheon International Airport, which are designed to help any passengers in need of important flight information or other assistance. The robots speak four languages (Korean, English, Japanese and Chinese, which were found to be the four most popular languages spoken at Incheon airport) and can escort passengers to their correct departure gate with a quick scan of their boarding pass or bring them to the closest restaurants or other facilities. In the same month, LG also launched similar-looking airport cleaning robots at Incheon airport, which can detect the areas of the airport that need the most cleaning work and can calculate the most efficient routes to reach these areas.

Also in 2019, the country started testing a proposed driverless bus system that could summon a local bus to your desired location with a tap on your smartphone touchscreen. Developed by KTI, Hyundai Motor Co., and SK Telecom Co. in collaboration with Seoul University, a test run of a 15-seat autonomous bus was said to have successfully changed lanes and stopped in front of crosswalks in the presence of other cars. The system is designed to be especially useful for the elderly and people with disabilities. If all goes well in the testing phase, these driverless buses are slated to be introduced on a preliminary level in Sejong by around 2022, before being rolled out in other regions.

Artificial intelligence (AI) is reportedly either already in use or being planned for use by around one quarter of the country's top 137 corporations for their hiring processes, according to the Korea Economic Research Institute (KERI). These AI video-hiring systems are said to measure a range of capabilities, including problem-solving, through a series of tests that are designed to be like games and can't be solved by memorizing a set of facts. The system has been used widely enough to have seen several people attend cram schools to learn how to prepare for job interviews that use an AI hiring process.

The future of technology in South Korea is poised to include flying taxis that take off and land vertically, driverless cars controlled by facial recognition and human look-alike AI robots capable of forming memories and hundreds of facial expressions. These were some of the state-of-the-art technologies revealed to be in development among South Korea's tech giants at the Consumer Electronics Show (CES), the world's biggest technology trade show, in 2020.

The country had its largest number of exhibitors in 2020, with nearly 400 companies including Samsung, LG and Hyundai. There were also more than 200 tech startup companies, which is a nearly 70 percent increase in number on the year before, demonstrating the pace at which the tech industry is exploding in South Korea. The country boasted the third highest number of exhibitors, just behind the US and China.

South Korea's technology industry has also been expanding beyond the consumer sector. In January 2020, the Korea Aerospace Research Institute also revealed its first-ever locally constructed space rocket is slated to launch in 2021. The Nuri rocket is capable of carrying a 1.5 ton satellite into low orbit and was said to be undergoing various tests at the Naro Space Center in Goheung in the Jeollonamdo province.

K Lifestyle

K Beauty

Origins and perception of beauty

A few years ago when I was in South Korea, I had an encounter with an uncle of mine whose first words upon seeing me for the first time in about 25 years weren't 'hello' or 'how are you' but rather 'What's happened to your skin? You used to have such white porcelain skin as a little girl ... you're darker now', referring to my tanned skin at the time, which I'd earned from my travels around some sunnier parts of the world in the months prior to my visit.

As unceremonious as that reunion was, it was a poignant reminder of the difference in the perception of beauty in Korean culture compared with Western society. The preference for (or, in some cases, obsession over) pale, ivory skin over a sun-kissed glow is prevalent in South Korea, stemming from what was considered beautiful throughout history in not only Korea but also much of East Asia.

Women of the wealthier upper classes all had pale skin because they remained indoors, rather than working outside in the field on farms under the scorching sun, as the women of the lower classes did. Having pale skin, therefore, was not only considered more beautiful but also denoted a higher social ranking.

Pale skin has also remained preferable among Korean women because most are very conscious of the damaging effects of the sun. In South Korea, you won't see anyone sunning themselves at the beach under direct sunlight and instead most will be covering themselves, particularly their faces, under hats and parasols.

The secret to ageless Korean skin

I always hear friends and even strangers comment on how Asian women tend to look nearly frozen in time, with youthful looking skin. So, what's the secret behind this ageless beauty? Part of the answer to that is that it's down to our mothers. One of the reasons I look young (or I've been told I do, at least) is down to genetics because my mother also looks much younger than her age. But having the young gene doesn't mean I can kick back and never worry about my skin. While growing up, I've learned the importance of skincare from watching my own mother look after her skin and I think this is true for many Korean women.

Skincare is a big industry in South Korea but it's also a big part of its tradition. Your skin has always been considered a prized possession that needs to be taken care of and protected. Throughout history, the condition of your skin (especially in historic times when there was not much makeup to enhance your looks) was one of the key, if not only, measures of women's beauty in society. So skin has always been an important part of the physical body.

One of the most basic beauty regimens of Korean women is sun protection. You'll find that many women, from young to old, always wear some form of cover to protect their skin from sun damage. This is probably the biggest reason why Korean women tend to have youthful skin even as they get older, on top of being helped by genes passed down from their mothers. Korean skincare products also tend to be made with mostly natural ingredients. You'll see so many different face masks made with various different types of food – from black sesame to potato and seaweed – on the market. The roots of this can also be traced back in history when ingredients such as ground mung beans mixed with water were used as soap, while lotions were made from the juice of plants like aloe vera.

Today, vitamin E is a big component of healthy skincare and it's been a personal staple of mine for years – a tip I give whenever people ask me about my own skincare. But during Korea's dynasty eras, women also used to apply safflower oil to their face, which is high in vitamin E.

Korean women have also benefited from a beauty industry that has been much ahead of the curve in terms of cosmetic research and technology. Koreans introduced BB creams (blemish balm creams) to the Western market in around 2011–12 and it has since opened the West to the K-beauty industry. BB creams and CC (colour control) creams were new products in the Western world but these had been used in Korea for years. They were only starting to be marketed globally at the time and have been exploding since.

Several retailers like TK Maxx and Primark have even introduced a K-beauty range, which was said to have flown off the shelves when it first hit the market. The Korean government, including the Ministry of Food and Drug Safety, has been supportive of the continued research and development of the Korean cosmetic industry, which has allowed it to thrive and be the global business it has become today.

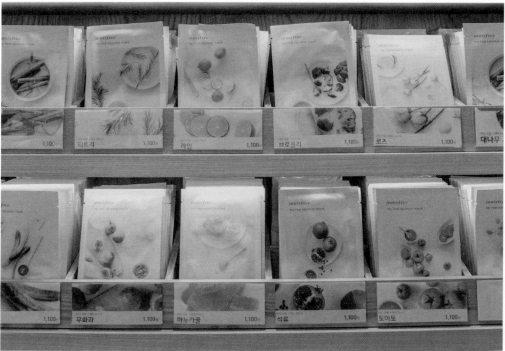

Top Korean skincare tips

Koreans reportedly spend twice as much money on makeup as Americans. It's a reflection of how much Koreans value and truly invest in their skin. Korean skincare rituals may involve several steps but it's like giving yourself a quick mini-facial every morning and night, so I enjoy the calming aspect of this. It also forces you to slow down physically and mentally at least once or twice a day to focus on self-care, which can be beneficial to your wellbeing. The number of steps in the routine varies according to the individual but it would be fair to say most daily regimens involve 10 steps, more or less. The following are some basic daily rituals for healthy skin practised by many Koreans.

Never sleep with makeup on: regardless of how late I get home or how tired I am, I always use a makeup remover to properly remove makeup from my skin. Oil-based makeup removers are better if you wear a lot of makeup, but otherwise water-based removers will work well.

Wash your face with a cleanser: even if your makeup remover says your face doesn't require washing after use, do always wash your face with a facial cleanser afterwards. This second round of cleansing removes any residual impurities on the face and is something that Korean women swear by. During the mornings, rinse your face with cold water to get the blood flowing but also to tighten the pores. At night, wash your face with warm water to open up the pores to remove dirt and impurities. This will also allow hydration of your pores and better absorption of the skincare products you'll be applying.

Exfoliate: a key part of the weekly regimen is to remove all dead skin cells using an exfoliating cream, gel or mask, twice a week. I find a charcoal or clay mask to be soothing and cleansing at the same time.

Slap your face: one distinct practice I've grown up watching during my own mother's skincare routine is that she would slap the product onto her face, rather than just rubbing it. Slapping your face (firm enough to actually make a noise but not enough to cause pain or leave marks) helps the product penetrate deeper into the skin for better absorption. Slapping also increases blood

ABOVE LEFT: A customer picks out hand cream in the Myeongdong shopping district in Seoul.
BELOW LEFT: Korean facial sheet masks from comestic brand Innisfree.

circulation through your face, leaving you with a naturally youthful rosy glow, while firming your face muscles and reducing any sagging. I love that it also helps wake me up in the mornings.

Apply toner: using toner is key for helping your skin to better absorb products applied afterwards. It's best to apply toner as soon as you've come out of the shower or washed your face to quickly lock in the moisture in your skin.

Apply an essence, serum or ampoule: use an essence product after your toner to add another layer of hydration to the skin before you apply serum. Serums contain a high concentration of active ingredients that target specific problems on the skin, from pigmentation to wrinkles, while an ampoule is a super-concentrated serum. Serums and essence can be applied daily, while an ampoule should be used only temporarily to treat certain skin conditions.

Put on a sheet mask: sheet masks have been all the rage in Korea for a while. These thin sheets applied to the face come in a variety of textures, from cloth to rubber, and are made with various ingredients that offer different benefits – from hydration to brightening of the complexion. Wearing times differ but most are worn for around 15–20 minutes. Storing masks in the fridge keeps them cool and makes them more rejuvenating when you apply to your face.

Apply eye cream: no matter how amazing your skin may be, tired-looking eyes with dark circles will always age you, so eye cream is a must to keep the eye area as bright and wrinkle-free as possible.

Seal the skin with a moisturiser: this is the thickest of the layers applied to your face in the regimen, so it's the final step to seal in moisture within your face.

Less is more

As with other aspects of Korean culture, especially during the Joseon Dynasty, its definition of beauty was linked to Confucian beliefs, stressing inner over outer beauty and favouring a clean, healthy-looking face. The middle and upper classes wore lighter makeup, while courtesans in the royal courts known as *gisaeng* (기생) wore bolder, more colourful makeup. But even *gisaengs* used makeup powder to make their skin look pale, as opposed to looking darker.

Growing up, my mother would tell me that makeup needs to be subtle and elegant. If she ever saw me wearing dark red lipstick or other strikingly bright makeup, she would half-jokingly say that I looked like a *gisaeng*. So, a natural style of makeup or seeming like you're not wearing any makeup at all is the key trend among Koreans. Even the way makeup is applied is done to look as natural as possible, such as with lipstick. Most Korean women go for a stained lip look, achieved by gently patting the lipstick onto their lips rather than rolling on multiple, thick layers to create a colourful darker lip.

The world capital of plastic surgery

The focus on the importance of beauty and highly idealized beauty standards in South Korea has made it the global capital for plastic surgery. The country is said to have the highest per capita rate of plastic surgery in the world, with reportedly nearly a million procedures performed every year. It's no surprise that South Korea ranks among the top five countries in the world with the highest number of plastic surgeons, according to a 2018 survey by the International Society of Aesthetic Plastic Surgery.

Some of the most popular procedures in South Korea include the double eye-lid surgery to create larger-looking eyes and jaw-shaving to create a V-shaped chin and, ultimately, a smaller face. Many young Koreans aspire to look like K-pop stars and other celebrities who maintain polished public images that perpetuate unrealistic beauty standards. Many of these celebrities have had to undergo surgery to achieve a certain look in the hopes of increasing their chance of success in the celebrity world.

In South Korea and some other Asian countries, you can even buy 'face lifting tapes', which are translucent strips of tape placed along the cheeks to pull back the face to help create contours and the illusion of higher cheekbones. Makeup can then be applied over the face tape.

Cosmetic surgery in South Korea has become a social norm and you'll see lots of large wall-sized billboards within metro stations and other public spaces advertising various plastic surgery clinics. Many of these are in the Gangnam district of Seoul along what's said to be called the 'beauty belt', where you'll find around 400 or so plastic surgery clinics within just one square mile.

Not every person with seemingly 'perfect' physical features in Korea has undergone surgery. There are plenty of people with naturally amazing features and there's certainly a lot to learn from the country's influential skincare industry.

K Fashion

Koreans are an imaginative bunch and fashion here comes in many forms, from street style or casual sporty to more formal looks among the older working crowd. Koreans are very fashion-conscious, especially the youth in urban areas. Fashionistas can be seen at Seoul Fashion Week, which is held in the Dongdaemun Design Plaza, a sprawling complex that is great for people-watching and catching a glimpse of the talented fashion brains in the capital.

Fashion trends differ according to age group and taste, but the younger generation in Korea seems to be more expressive with a clear point of view in their fashion choices. The fact that young people influence fashion trends the most makes it more attainable and accessible to a wider audience. The fashion world is not put in an elitist light or exclusive in the way that it might be in fashion capitals like Paris, where you might feel snubbed by those in the inner circles of fashion if you aren't dressed head to toe in designer labels.

Seoul Fashion Week can easily be attended by purchasing a ticket, whereas in New York, London or Paris, getting a seat at fashion week is like pulling a star from the sky, to use the Korean proverb. There it's all about knowing the right people to be invited to attend these shows, but this isn't necessarily the case in South Korea.

How to dress like a Korean

Luxury brands don't always dictate the most popular styles. Not everyone in Korea walks around in Chanel couture or carrying Louis Vuitton bags. But plenty of people know how to dress the part, even without all the labels, and that goes for both women and men.

Koreans have a touch of cuteness in their personality and it definitely comes out in their style, whether it be something as subtle as a hair accessory or more obvious like a large hat, even if the rest of their outfit might not be overly cute in style. But generally speaking, most Koreans follow a minimalist style with one or two accents – which could be an accessory or pattern, or something else – to add a unique touch.

The K-pop fashion scene is a bit different from the average street-wear look because K-pop stars tend to exude a slightly sexier, more provocative style – think tight jeans, body-con dresses and short shorts with low cut shirts and crop tops – than the quirkier styles you might see on the street.

Fashionistas arrive at Seoul Fashion Week at Dongdaemun Design Plaza in 2019.

While the young professional working crowd sticks to more formal suits and dresses, even formal work-wear features some unique cuts and lines, so there isn't really a standard classic-cut suit or skirt suit.

The looks I highlight below are meant for achieving casual Korean street-style outfits for everyday wear. These are just some observations I've made over the years. How you put these items together will create your unique style.

Neutrals and pastels: many Koreans favour lighter shades and neutral, earth tones as the base for their outfits. Some might accentuate their neutral outfit with a small pop of colour somewhere or with a striped top or a shirt with wording across it.

Oversized sweatshirts and cardigans: loose-fitting tops are more prevalent than tight fits among youth.

Loose jeans: not the extremely baggy style of the 1990s, but generally looser trousers are more on trend than more skintight styles.

K LIFESTYLE

Larger hair pins: bigger, bolder hair pins, which might entail crystal studs, glittery trims or floral shapes, started appearing among the crowds at fashion weeks around the world in the past year or so, but these sparkling hair accessories have been a favourite among Korean girls for a while.

A-line skirts and shorts: these are popular among Korean women, both short and long styles. They help accentuate the waist of boxy frames and are easily paired with oversized t-shirts and cardigans.

Sportswear: casual sporty and sporty-chic styles are common on the street among youth, so you'll see lots of caps, bomber jackets, hoodies and trainers – sometimes paired with more formal layers like trench coats.

Chunky trainers: lots of women wear trainers with thick platform-style soles, paired with straight leg trousers or flowy long skirts and mini-skirts.

ABOVE: Contemporary Korean fashion on show in Seoul.

K health and wellness

Average life expectancy for South Koreans has increased dramatically over the past few decades. Just before the country's economic boom around 1960, life expectancy was at 52.4 years (a whopping 26 years below the average figure for other countries that are part of the OECD). But by 2005, life expectancy jumped to 78.5 years (the average among OECD countries), which indicates an increase of around six months every year between 1960 and 2005 – the greatest leap any OECD country has ever had, according to a study published in the American Journal of Public Health.

But fast forward to more recent times and it seems to be only getting better. A new study in 2017 by *The Lancet* revealed that by 2030, South Korea is projected to become the first country in the world to have a life expectancy that is greater than 90 years. The study indicates there is a 90 percent chance that South Korean women in 2030 will live more than 86–87 years and a 57 percent probability that life expectancy will be higher than 90 years.

The study also predicted that there is a 95-percent chance that South Korean men will live beyond 80 years in 2030, and a more than 27-percent chance that South Korean men's life expectancy will surpass 85 years.

The high life projections for South Korea has been driven by the expected decline in death from infection and chronic diseases, as well as continued decrease in infant mortality. Expected improvement in childhood nutrition has also played a part – South Korea, as well as Japan, were reported to have seen the largest gains in adult height over the past century, according to the study. South Koreans were also found to have maintained lower body-mass index and blood pressure than most Western countries and lower instances of smoking among women.

Clearly South Koreans are doing something right, whether it be consciously or not, if the life expectancy projections are this positive. So, what is the secret to their health?

6 secrets to a healthy life

Korean diet: two Korean staples (*kimchee* and tofu) have contributed to the long-term health of Koreans and South Korea was the first country in the world to cultivate soy. Soy beans have enormous health benefits, while fermented foods are good for gut health. Many Korean foods like *kimchee* and other pickled vegetables are fermented.

Koreans may also be healthier than others because they naturally use a lot of vegetables in their native dishes and sugar was historically not in their diet because it was a luxury item. Sugar was also used less, as traditionally most food needed to be preserved, since there were no refrigerators in farming communities, so a lot of food was pickled, fermented and salted to give it a longer shelf life.

***Jjimjilbangs* and hot springs:** a *jjimjilbang* (찜질방), a Korean sauna, is a very quintessential Korean experience. My memories of visiting them as a little girl don't recall a particularly glamorous space but today there are lots of luxury saunas and spas, where many Koreans like to go for a day of relaxation. Sitting in these heated facilities offers immense health benefits, such as lower blood pressure and a reduced risk of heart disease and diabetes. Koreans are known to make regular visits to *jjimjilbangs* for a good scrub and cleansing session but also as a way of bonding when accompanied by a friend/family member or two. There are also plenty of natural hot springs worth seeking out on a longer excursion outside the capital for the benefit of the cleaner mountain air.

Korean medicine: the practice of Korean medicine can be traced back to around 3,000 BC during the Neolithic Age, when bone and stone needles were said to have been discovered in the Hamgyeong Province, located in present-day North Korea. Much of the earliest medicine in Korea was based on ancient Chinese medicine. During the Koryŏ Dynasty, there was a focus on the study of medicinal herbs native to Korea but medical theories and books published around this time were still based mostly on Chinese medicine from China's Song Dynasty.

LEFT: Traditional medicinal herbs on sale at a street market in Seoul.

It was during the Joseon Dynasty that the Korean medicine field developed most, trying to break away from Chinese influence, and a few medical encyclopedias were published such as the *Hyangyak Jipseongbang* (향약집성방, 1433), which featured 703 Korean native medicines.

Hanyak: many Koreans like to maintain their health with various forms of *hanyak* (한약) – Korean traditional herbal medicine – and other Chinese herbal treatments. Some parents have their young high-school children take *boyak* (보약), a type of *hanyak*, to strengthen them for their studies, especially those in their last year preparing for the dreaded university entrance examinations. *Boyak* is a liquid tonic brewed from a mix of different herbs and roots. It is considered a luxury health supplement that many parents have either their children or elderly grandparents consume for its supposed benefits.

Eastern medicine focuses on achieving balance in *qi* (life force energy) throughout the body and *boyak* targets restoring balance when there is either a deficiency or overabundance in the amount of *qi* required across your organs to maintain healthy levels of functionality. Symptoms of being deficient include cold hands and a cold stomach, feeling lethargic and extremely tired, as well as digestive issues.

Many Koreans take *boyak* to help restore their energy balance and some take it as a preventative measure, especially ahead of or during the colder months. But *boyak* can also be beneficial in the summer when you are prone to sweating a lot, which causes an overexertion of energy. *Boyak* helps to remedy that imbalance in *qi*. It also helps to give you the energy needed for your pores to close up and reduce the amount that you perspire in hot weather.

There is no ideal time to take *boyak* but it's best for whenever you feel very low in energy. Each *boyak* tonic is unique to the patient's needs and prescribed according to exactly what type of energy balance correction is needed in whichever part of the body, depending on the patient's symptoms.

Acupuncture: this practice is based on the notion of correcting an imbalance of *qi* by applying pressure along certain points on the body's various meridians, which are lines along which *qi* is said to run. Among the most common types of Korean acupuncture practised is Saam, which focuses on 12 specific types of *qi* that run along 12 meridians. Needles are used to apply pressure at one of five points to address any deficiencies or overabundance in *qi*.

Among the newest forms of Korean acupuncture is herbal acupuncture, which involves the injection of a highly potent herbal extract or highly purified bee venom at certain pressure points. This has reportedly helped relieve chronic symptoms including back and shoulder pain, headaches, rheumatoid arthritis, osteoarthritis, as well as helping with diabetes and obesity.

Medical tourism: another reason for Korean good health may be that healthcare is free to all citizens, as well as foreign nationals, and is funded by a national health insurance scheme.

Private healthcare is also believed to be around 20–30 percent of the price for the same treatment in Europe or the US and also much cheaper than in its neighbouring Asian countries such as Japan, China and parts of Southeast Asia. The country boasts some of the best medical facilities in the world because of its existing cutting-edge technology sector, which makes it all the more value for money. There has been a rise in medical tourism to the country in recent years.

The government's Ministry of Health supports the medical tourism sector, with information centres set up in various cities including in the capital Seoul (such as the Gangnam Medical Tour Center, which guides you to some of the best clinics in Gangnam) as well as in Daegu, Busan, Daejon and even at the arrivals lounge of Incheon International Airport.

South Korea specializes in skincare and plastic surgery. Its advanced medical research and technology, as well as state-of-the-art facilities, have allowed it to provide some of the top-rated healthcare for complex disorders and procedures such as cancer, cardiovascular and spinal diseases, coronary artery bypass, coronary angioplasty, hip replacements and transplants. The number of patients in the country who have reported five-year cancer survival rates for various cancers (including thyroid, stomach, breast, liver, colon and pancreatic) has been higher than in the US, Canada and Japan, according to figures from the country's National Cancer Information Center.

K homes

Historically Koreans lived in *hanoks* (한옥), which are traditional homes with either thatched roofing or ceramic tile roofs, the latter being more common for *hanoks* that housed noblemen. They were first built during the Joseon Dynasty and many of the most historic ones were destroyed following the Korean War. There are several *hanok* villages dotted around the country where you can explore these houses (see page 54).

The typical Korean home

Hanoks were considered to be very environmentally friendly and generally better for your health because their construction was entirely from natural materials. This may provide another explanation as to why Koreans were and continue to be healthy, having the good genes from their ancestors who lived in these healthy homes.

From the wooden flooring and wooden pillars to the paper used to cover doors and window frames which was made from tree pulp, the natural materials also made *hanoks* much more breathable and cooler in the summer, while the clay roofing of the ceramic tiles acted as a heat insulator in the winter. Another unique feature of *hanoks* is *ondol* (온돌) underfloor heating, where a slab of stone is placed beneath the floor and heated from an

ABOVE: The exterior of a traditional Korean *hanok*.

outside furnace using wood smoke or charcoal. The heat is released slowly from the stone and transfers to the room and the rest of the home.

The position of *hanoks* was also important and they were built according to the principle of *baesanimsu* (배산임수), which says the ideal spot for a house is to have a mountain behind it and a river in front of it, so that it would be windproof from the harsh winter winds coming from the north and have easy access to water.

Hanoks have mostly been replaced by apartment complexes and Western-style structures in modern times. But the tradition of removing your shoes when entering a home, which was said to have begun with the introduction of *hanoks* and *ondol* heating, remains. Many people wear house slippers at home and keep their shoes near the door inside their house or apartment.

Many traditional families, especially the older generation, living in older country-style homes prefer to sleep on the floor over thick bedding, which is the traditional way of sleeping. The bedding is folded up and stored away in the dresser when not sleeping. Many also use cylindrical round pillows, instead of the square, flat pillows seen in Western homes.

In many smaller homes, leisure activities such as having a meal or chatting over a cup of tea are still done while sitting on the floor, so several floor mats are usually available for guests to sit on. But, of course, larger Western-style modern homes have sofas and beds, so floor mats aren't used.

Bathrooms in many Korean homes tend to have a drain on the floor, similar to a wet room, so often there is no separate shower or bath. But Western-style homes, usually in upmarket areas, may have a separate bath/shower in the bathroom, even if the floor has a drain. The wet-room design is mostly for practical purposes. Having a drain makes it easier to clean the entire bathroom using the shower spray, without worrying about flooding the bathroom. People tend to wear shower slippers in these wet-room-style bathrooms, as the floor inevitably gets wet and slippery while bathing or cleaning.

Large modern homes in wealthy neighbourhoods may have a small front garden (usually found just after you enter the main front gate of the home) in the form of a grass patch with a small table and chairs for hosting guests. But traditional-style homes tend to have an open *madang* (마당), a small empty courtyard space.

Historically, *hanoks* had empty *madangs* that served as a space for housework or hosting events/ceremonies or even just as a play area for kids. *Hanoks* were all about being mindful of and non-disturbing towards their natural surroundings. So keeping this space empty was also in line with the minimalist, environmentally friendly aesthetic, instead of carving out a garden or building another structure on the ground to fill the courtyard.

Traditional gardens that you might think of in the suburbs of Western countries are not prevalent in Korean homes because the suburbs don't really exist in South Korea, so there isn't the space. Most residential areas either tend to be in cities, so urban with high-rise apartments and smaller homes, or rural, surrounded by farmland. Owning a swanky apartment or spacious home in an urban setting is seen more as living the dream in Korean society, than owning a house in the countryside, as many urban-dwellers in Western societies might aspire to achieve.

Making your home more Korean

Korean homes tend to take a minimalist, understated approach, maximizing space over aesthetics with natural lighting and making use of natural materials, in a nod to the past, when these materials were the most readily available.

Many Korean homes might incorporate some Korean pottery, which dates back to around 8000 BC. Among the most popular native Korean earthenware are celadons, which are glazed pots featuring a vibrant jade-green colour that were developed during the Koryŏ Dynasty. Ceramics from the Koryŏ era are noted to have a refined elegance, with detailing depicting nature but earthenware from the Joseon Dynasty, such as pear-shaped white porcelain pots, have a more modest and minimalist design, which reflected the principles of the Confucian state that dominated government and society at the time. You might see either type of Korean ceramic on display on shelves or corner tables in modern Korean homes with a traditional touch.

Many traditional-style homes today also feature a wall-sized folding paper screen along a wall of the main bedroom or in the living room. These screens can feature panels with Korean writing, embroidery or paintings of flowers and other natural landscapes. They were common in many houses of the Korean upper classes and can be a subtle Korean vintage statement piece in your home.

RIGHT: The traditional Korean way of sleeping is to lie on thick bedding on the floor.

Picture credits

All illustrations by Good Studio. All photographic images appear courtesy of the companies and individuals listed below. We apologise in advance for any unintentional omissions or errors and will be pleased to insert the appropriate acknowledgement to any companies or individuals in any subsequent edition of this work.

1 Jason Yoder/Alamy Stock Photo; 2–3 Alex Veprik/Getty Images; 4–5 Time, Life/Getty Images; 6–7 Diego Mariottini/EyeEm/Getty Images; 8–9 Sang Taek Jang/Eyeem/Getty Images; 13 Tibor Bognar/ Alamy Stock Photo; 15 Eric Lafforgue/Alamy Stock Photo; 17 Hemis/Alamy Stock Photo; 19 Vaughan/ Stringer/Hulton Archive/Getty Images; 20–21 Xinhua/Alamy Stock Photo; 23 Soo Kim; 24 top Phillip Bond/Alamy Stock Photo; 24 bottom Olaf Schuelke/Alamy Stock Photo; 27 Keystone-France/ Contributor/Getty Images; 30 Kate Hockenhull/Alamy Stock Photo; 32–33 Bloomberg/Contributor/Getty Images; 34–35 Wang Jingqiang/Xinhua/Alamy Live News; 36–37 Noppasin Wongchum/Alamy Stock Photo; 39 Getty Images Entertainment; 41 Busan Drone/Alamy Stock Photo; 44–45 David Ducoin/Getty Images; 46 top left Jon Arnold Images Ltd/Alamy Stock Photo; 46 top right Nicolas McComber/Getty Images; 46 bottom Lee Kyung Jun/Imazins/Getty Images; 48 Gavin Hellier/Alamy Stock Photo; 49 Yooran Park/Alamy Stock Photo; 50–51 Derek Teo/Alamy Stock Photo; 52 Noppasin Wongchum/Alamy Stock Photo; 54–55 Prasit photo/Getty Images; 56–57; Alex Veprik/Getty Images; 58 Busan Drone/Alamy Stock Photo; 60 top Gim Seng Tan/500px/Getty Images; 60 bottom Mariusz Prusaczyk/Alamy Stock Photo; 62–63 SIRIOH Co., LTD/Alamy Stock Photo; 64–65 Eric Hevesy/Getty Images; 66–67 Eric Hevesy/Getty Images; 69 Sungjin Kim/Getty Images; 70 Juergen Ritterbach/Alamy Stock Photo; 72 Dmitry Rukhlenko – Travel Photos/Alamy Stock Photo; 74 Kim Kaminski/Alamy Stock Photo; 75 Images & Stories/Alamy Stock Photo; 76 top Manfred Gottschalk/Getty images; 76 bottom Simon Reddy/Alamy Stock Photo; 79 Jon Arnold Images Ltd/Alamy Stock Photo; 80 Kadek Bonit Permadi/Stockimo/Alamy Stock Photo; 82 Eddie Gerald/Alamy Stock Photo; 87 Jung Yeon-Je/Getty Images; 89 Yelim Lee/Stringer/Getty Images; 92–93 Chung Sung-Jun/Getty Images; 94 Carlo Bollo/Alamy Stock Photo; 102 Eddie Gerald/Alamy Stock Photo; 106 Sean Pavone/Alamy Stock Photo; 109 Insung Jeon/Getty Images; 110 top Ed Jones/Getty Images; 110 bottom left Cultura RM/Alamy Stock Photo; 110 bottom right Michele Burgess/Alamy Stock Photo; 111 Stockbyte/Getty Images; 112 Chung Sung-Jun/Getty Images; 113 ZUMA Press/Alamy Stock Photo; 114 © Magnolia Pictures/Courtesy Everett Collection; 117 left Tom Purslow/Getty Images; 117 right Darling Archive/Alamy Stock Photo; 121 Chad Ehlers/Alamy Stock Photo; 123 Oleg Zartdinov/ Shutterstock; 126 Jarrod Hall/Alamy Stock Photo; 129 Maria S. / Alamy Stock Photo; 130–131 Seksan Manee/Alamy Stock Photo; 135 Ed Jones/AFP via Getty Images; 136 Hotsum/Shutterstock; 137 TongRo Images/Alamy Stock Photo; 141 top Alisher Irismetov/Shutterstock; 141 bottom left Alisher Irismetov/ Shutterstock; 141 bottom right Alisher Irismetov/Shutterstock; 142 Chung Sung-Jun/Getty Images; 144 Ed Jones/AFP via Getty Images; 147 Loes Kieboom/Alamy Stock Photo; 148–149 Tawatchai Prakobkit/ Alamy Stock Photo; 152 top B Christopher/Alamy Stock Photo; 152 bottom Saran Poroong/Alamy Stock Photo; 155 Architecture Firm: ArchiWorkshop/Architects: Hee-Jun Sim, Su-Jeong Park/Photograph: June-Young Lim; 157 Nigel Hicks/Alamy Stock Photo; 159 Olivier Prevosto/Onze/Icon Sport/Getty Images; 163 Mirtmirt/Shutterstock; 164 Norikko/Shutterstock; 166 Me Darat/Shutterstock; 168 Simon Reddy/ Alamy Stock Photo; 170 F. Cortes-Cabanillas/Alamy Stock Photo; 174 SIRIOH Co., LTD/Alamy Stock Photo; 183 Kim Jae-Hwan/AFP via Getty Images; 184 top Photo by Terence Patrick/CBS via Getty Images; 184 bottom Starship Entertainment; 189 Curzon Artificial Eye/Kobal/Shutterstock; 190 Kevin Winter/Getty Images; 191 top Moho/Kobal/Shutterstock; 191 bottom Chungeorahm Film/Kobal/ Shutterstock; 194 Wikicommons; 195 REDA & Co srl/Michele Bella/Alamy Stock Photo; 196 All-a-Shutter/ Alamy Stock Photo; 199 Newscom/Alamy Stock Photo; 206 top SeongJoon Cho/Bloomberg via Getty Images; 206 bottom Luoxi/Alamy Stock Photo; 211 left Photo by Christian Vierig/Getty Images; 211 right Photo by Christian Vierig/Getty Images; 212 WENN Rights Ltd/Alamy Stock Photo; 214 Robert Coy/ Alamy Stock Photo; 218 Smyungku Kim/Shutterstock; 221 SIRIOH Co., LTD/Alamy Stock Photo

About the author

Soo Kim is a reporter for *Newsweek* (an international news publication), covering the latest in travel and culture from the London bureau. She studied international journalism at City, University of London before working as a reporter and commissioning editor for the travel section of the *Daily Telegraph* (a UK national newspaper) from 2010–2019. She grew up in New York City, where she worked before moving to London.

Follow Soo on Twitter (@MissSooKim) and Instagram (@miss.soo.kim).

Acknowledgements

Of all the pages I've had to write for this book, somehow this one felt most difficult to begin, not knowing how to start and where to end, with too many acknowledgements to be made in between.

But my first thanks must go to White Lion Publishing for approaching me with this unique book project, which came to me at such an opportune moment in my life and career, as if the stars had aligned. It has been a true labour of love and an ode to all the reasons why I adore and am so proud of my Korean heritage and culture.

Many thanks especially to Pete Jorgensen and Julia Shone for being so collaborative, efficient and easy to work with from the onset and making this such a smooth, seamless and enjoyable creative process.

My utmost thanks to the production and design team for creating the beautiful pages of this book and to all the other staff members who made this project come together (even amid a pandemic).

To my dear mother 김 여사님 (my biggest fan), father 김 선생님 and brother M.K. 오빠: thank you for your love and support 항상 감싸주고 기둥이 된 우리 가족, 우리 엄마 아빠, 키워 주셔서 감사합니다.

To each of my dearest friends (you know who you are): thank you for your patient ears, strength, comfort and unwavering belief in me on this epic journey called life.

And last, but not least, to my readers: thank you so very much for your interest. I hope this book inspires you to further explore all things Korean.

Brimming with creative inspiration, how-to projects and useful information to enrich your everyday life, Quarto Knows is a favourite destination for those pursuing their interests and passions. Visit our site and dig deeper with our books into your area of interest: Quarto Creates, Quarto Cooks, Quarto Homes, Quarto Lives, Quarto Drives, Quarto Explores, Quarto Gifts, or Quarto Kids.

First published in 2020 by White Lion Publishing,
an imprint of The Quarto Group.
The Old Brewery, 6 Blundell Street
London, N7 9BH,
United Kingdom
T (0)20 7700 6700
www.QuartoKnows.com

ISBN 978 0 71125 709 2
Ebook ISBN 978 0 71125 710 8

10 9 8 7 6 5 4 3 2 1

Design by Ginny Zeal
Illustrations by Good Studio

Printed in China